THE BRAND GAP

THE BR/

AND GAP

HOW TO BRIDGE THE DISTANCE BETWEEN BUSINESS STRATEGY AND DESIGN

A WHITEBOARD OVERVIEW BY **MARTY NEUMEIER**

THE BRAND GAP (REVISED EDITION)

HOW TO BRIDGE THE DISTANCE BETWEEN BUSINESS STRATEGY AND DESIGN

A WHITEBOARD OVERVIEW BY MARTY NEUMEIER

NEW RIDERS
1249 EIGHTH STREET
BERKELEY, CA 94710
510/524-2178
800/283-9444
510/524-2221 (FAX)

NEW RIDERS IS AN IMPRINT OF PEACHPIT, A DIVISION OF PEARSON EDUCATION

FIND US ON THE WORLD WIDE WEB AT: WWW.PEACHPIT.COM
TO REPORT ERRORS, PLEASE SEND A NOTE TO ERRATA@PEACHPIT.COM

PROJECT EDITOR:	PRODUCTION EDITOR:	INDEXER:	BOOK DESIGNER:
BECKY MORGAN	LUPE EDGAR	CHERYL LENSER	HEATHER MCDONALD

ISBN 0-321-34810-9

9

PRINTED AND BOUND IN THE UNITED STATES OF AMERICA

TO EILEEN, LA MAGICIENNE DE MON COEUR

PREFACE

A lot of people talk about it. Yet very few people understand it. Even fewer know how to manage it. Still, everyone wants it. What is it? Branding, of course—arguably the most powerful business tool since the spreadsheet.

In this book I've tried to present a 30,000-foot view of brand: what it is (and isn't), why it works (and doesn't), and, most importantly, how to bridge the gap between logic and magic to build a sustainable competitive advantage.

While most books on branding present an exhaustive (and sometimes exhausting) array of examples and studies to support their theses, here I've taken the opposite tack. By presenting the least amount of information necessary, and by using the shorthand of the conference room— illustrations, diagrams, and summaries—I hope to bring the big ideas of branding into sharp focus.

Your time is valuable, so my first goal is to give you a book you can finish in a short plane ride. My second goal is to give you powerful principles that will last a career.

—Marty Neumeier

CONTENTS

s une brand.

(THIS IS NOT A BRAND.)

INTRODUCTION

WHAT A BRAND ISN'T.

Let's start with a clean slate. If we wipe away some of the misconceptions about brand, we can make more room for its truths.

Ready?

First of all, a brand is not a logo. The term LOGO is short for LOGOTYPE, design-speak for a trademark made from a custom-lettered word (LOGOS is Greek for WORD). The term logo caught on with people because it sounds cool, but what people really mean is a trademark, whether the trademark is a logo, symbol, monogram, emblem, or other graphic device. IBM uses a monogram, for example, while Nike uses a symbol. Both are trademarks, but neither are logos. Clear? What really matters here is that a logo, or any other kind of trademark, is not the brand itself. It's merely a symbol for it.

Second, a brand is not a corporate identity system. An identity system is a 20th-century construct for controlling the use of trademarks and trade-dress elements on company publications, advertisements, stationery, vehicles, signage, and so on. Fifty years ago, lithography was the communication technology du jour; identity manuals were designed to dictate the sizes, colors, spacing, and architecture of the printed page. Today there's still a need for identity manuals and the visual consistency they bring. But consistency alone does not create a brand.

Finally, a brand is not a product. Marketing people often talk about managing their brands, but what they usually mean is managing their products, or the sales, distribution, and quality thereof. To manage a brand is to manage something much less tangible—an aura, an invisible layer of meaning that surrounds the product.

So what exactly is a brand?

A brand is a person's gut feeling about a product, service, or company. It's a GUT FEELING because we're all emotional, intuitive beings, despite our best efforts to be rational. It's a PERSON'S gut feeling, because in the end the brand is defined by individuals, not by companies, markets, or the so-called general public. Each person creates his or her own version of it. While companies can't control this process, they can influence it by communicating the qualities that make this product different than that product. When enough individuals arrive at the same gut feeling, a company can be said to have a brand. In other words, a brand is not what YOU say it is. It's what THEY say it is. A brand is a kind of Platonic ideal—a concept shared by society to identify a specific class of things. To use Plato's example, whenever we hear the word "horse" we visualize a majestic creature with four legs, a long tail, and a mane falling over a muscular neck, an impression of power and grace, and the knowledge that a person can ride long distances on its back. Individual horses may differ, but in our minds we still recognize their common "horseness." Looked at from the other side of the equation, when we add up the parts that make a horse, the total is distinctive enough so that we think HORSE, not COW or BICYCLE.

A brand, like Plato's horse, is an approximate—yet distinct—understanding of a product, service, or company. To compare a brand with its competitors, we only need to know what makes it different. Brand management is the management of differences, not as they exist on data sheets, but as they exist in the minds of people.

A BRAND IS NOT WHAT

YOU SAY IT IS.

IT'S WHAT

THEY SAY IT IS.

WHY IS BRAND SUDDENLY HOT?

The idea of brand has been around for at least 5,000 years. So why is it such a big deal now?

Because as our society has moved from an economy of mass production to an economy of mass customization, our purchasing choices have multiplied. We've become information-rich and time-poor. As a result, our old method of judging products—by comparing features and benefits— no longer works. The situation is exacerbated by competitors who copy each others' features as soon as they're introduced, and by advances in manufacturing that make quality issues moot.

Today we base our choices more on symbolic attributes. What does the product look like? Where is it being sold? What kind of people buy it? Which "tribe" will I be joining if I buy it? What does the cost say about its desirability? What are other people saying about it? And finally, who makes it? Because if I can trust the maker, I can buy it now and worry about it later. The degree of trust I feel towards the product, rather than an assessment of its features and benefits, will determine whether I'll buy this product or that product.

THERE ARE 1,349 CAMERAS ON THE MARKET.
HOW DO YOU DECIDE WHICH ONE TO BUY?

IN VERISIGN WE TRUST.

The history of American currency provides a good demonstration of how trust relates to branding. After the Revolutionary War, when paper money was reduced to a fortieth of its previous value, gold and silver were the only types of currency people could trust. It was nearly a hundred years before people were willing to accept Silver Certificates as a substitute for the real thing, even though the new bills were backed by metal reserves. It took another hundred years before we were ready to accept Federal Reserve Notes as a substitute for Silver Certificates. These weren't backed by reserves at all, but by pure faith in the brand called America. Now we've learned to trust in a system of credit

THE EVOLUTION OF CURRENCY MIRRORS THE EVOLUTION OF TRUST.

cards for a large percentage of our transactions. Will we soon be ready to accept international cyber-currency as an improvement on credit cards? Sure, if we can trust it.

Trust creation is a fundamental goal of brand design. The complex flourishes and intricate images employed in the design of the Silver Certificate were no accident—they were conscious attempts to encourage trust in what was little more than a symbol for money.

The concept of trust is equally important when we trade our currency—whether metal, paper, plastic, or cyber—for goods and services. Trust is the ultimate shortcut to a buying decision, and the bedrock of modern branding.

WHAT'S YOUR BRAND WORTH?

Can you place a dollar value on your company's brand? You can certainly try, and for some companies the estimates are astonishing. The brand consultancy Interbrand routinely publishes a list of the top 100 global brands by valuation. The leader today is Coca-Cola with a brand worth of nearly $70 billion, which accounts for more than 60% of its market capitalization. Halfway down the list is Xerox with a brand valuation of $6 billion—a whopping 93% of its market cap.

If a company's brand value is such a large part of its assets, why isn't it listed on the balance sheet? Good question. But while companies ponder this, they're already using brand values as tools to obtain financing, put a price on licensing deals, evaluate mergers and acquisitions, assess damages in litigation cases, and justify the price of their stock.

There's an old saying in business, "What gets measured gets done." As brands become more measurable, companies are focusing on ways to increase their value.

One way is to follow the example of currency: Use design to encourage trust.

COKE'S MARKET CAP, INCLUDING BRAND VALUE: $120 BILLION

WITHOUT THE BRAND, COKE'S GLASS WOULD BE HALF EMPTY.

COKE'S MARKET CAP, NOT INCLUDING BRAND VALUE: $50 BILLION

BRAND HAPPENS.

So far, the eye-opening valuations on Interbrand's list have happened as much by chance as by design. While the figures undoubtedly represent a huge investment in time, energy, money, and study, they're mostly a side effect of caring more about sales, service, quality, marketing, and the myriad other things that occupy a business. For most of us, brand happens while we're doing something else.

But what if you could isolate brand from those other endeavors? What if you could study it, measure it, manage it, and influence it, rather than just let it happen?

This is precisely what companies are trying to do. They're appointing brand managers, who are building brand departments, which are populated by brand strategists, who are armed with brand research. What they're discovering, however, is that it takes more than strategy to build a brand. It takes strategy and creativity together.

Which brings us to the premise of this book.

THE BRAND GAP.

Strategy and creativity, in most companies, are separated by a mile-wide chasm. On one side are the strategists and marketing people who favor left-brain thinking—analytical, logical, linear, concrete, numerical, verbal. On the other side are the designers and creative people who favor right-brain thinking—intuitive, emotional, spatial, visual, physical.

Unfortunately, the left brain doesn't always know what the right brain is doing. Whenever there's a rift between strategy and creativity—between logic and magic—there's a brand gap. It can cause a brilliant strategy to fail where it counts most, at the point of contact with the customer, or it can doom a bold creative initiative before it's even launched, way back at the planning stage.

The gulf between strategy and creativity can divide a company from its customers so completely that no significant communication passes between them. For the customer, it can be like trying to listen to a state-of-the-art radio through incompatible speakers: The signal comes in strong, but the sounds are unintelligible.

DOES THE LEFT BRAIN KNOW

WHAT THE RIGHT BRAIN IS DOING?

INTRODUCING THE CHARISMATIC BRAND.

There are two ways to look at the brand gap:
1) it creates a natural barrier to communication,
and 2) it creates a natural barrier to competition.
Companies who learn how to bridge the gap have
a tremendous advantage over those who don't.
When brand communication comes through intact—
crystal clear and potent—it goes straight into people's brains without distortion, noise, or the need
to think too much about it. It shrinks the "psychic
distance" between companies and their constituents
so that a relationship can begin to develop. These
gap-crossing, distance-shrinking messages are
the building blocks of a charismatic brand.

You can tell which brands are charismatic,
because they're a constant topic in the cultural
conversation. Brands such as Coca-Cola, Apple,
Nike, IBM, Virgin, IKEA, BMW, and Disney have
become modern icons because they stand for
things that people want—i.e., joy, intelligence,
strength, success, comfort, style, motherly love,
and imagination. Smaller brands can also be charismatic. Companies such as John Deere, Google,
Cisco, Viking, Palm, Tupperware, and Trane all
exert a magnetic influence over their audiences.

When an AC contractor reads the tagline, "It's hard to stop a Trane," he thinks, "Damn straight."

A charismatic brand can be defined as any product, service, or company for which people believe there's no substitute. Not surprisingly, charismatic brands often claim the dominant position in their categories, with market shares of 50% or higher. They also tend to command the highest price premiums—up to 40% more than generic products or services. And, most importantly, they're the least likely to fall victim to commoditization.

Among the hallmarks of a charismatic brand are a clear competitive stance, a sense of rectitude, and a dedication to aesthetics. Why aesthetics? Because it's the language of feeling, and, in a society that's information-rich and time-poor, people value feeling more than information.

Aesthetics is so powerful that it can turn a commodity into a premium product. Don't believe me? Look at Morton. Ordinary table salt is the ultimate commodity—unless it has a little girl on the package.

There are no dull products, only dull brands. Any brand, backed by enough courage and imagination, can become a charismatic brand. But first you need to master the five disciplines of branding. →

1: DIFFEF

ENTIATE

2 : COLLA

BORATE

3 : INNOV

4:VALIDA

5 : CULTIV

DISCIPLINE 1 : DIFFERENTIATE

THREE LITTLE QUESTIONS.

Wanna bring a high-level marketing meeting to a screeching halt? Just do what brand consultant Greg Galle of Creative Capital does—demand unambiguous answers to three little questions:

1) Who are you?
2) What do you do?
3) Why does it matter?

Now, the first question is fairly easy for most companies to answer. "We're Global Grommets, a multinational provider of grommets." The second question is a little harder. "We make grommets— no, we make more than grommets, because we have a full line of widgets, too." But the third question, why it matters, can get sticky. "It matters because we make really good grommets—and widgets." (Sure, but everyone says that.) "Because we sell the widest selection of grommets and widgets." (Right, but I only need one kind of grommet, and I already buy it from someone else.) "Because we have the best people." (Yeah, right—prove it.) Unless you have compelling answers to all three questions, meaning that customers find them irresistible, you haven't got a brand. If you do have compelling answers, great—you can skip this chapter.

Still reading? Thought so. Because most companies have occasional trouble answering the first question, a little trouble answering the second, and a lot of trouble answering the third. Together, these questions provide a litmus test for what makes you different, what gives your company its raison d'etre.

A good example of a company that knows what it's about is John Deere. "We're John Deere. We make farm tractors and related equipment. It matters because generations of farmers have trusted our equipment." Their trademark is a silhouette of a leaping stag, and their tagline is "Nothing runs like a Deere." As long as the Deere folks can keep it this simple, their brand will keep running. If they begin to add too many UNRELATED products and services to their line, however, their message will turn muddy and their brand will get stuck. Let's say, for example, that they decide to hedge their bets by adding health care, real estate, and fertilizer to the mix. How would they then differentiate their brand? "We're John Deere. You know us for tractors, but we do much more. It matters because you can come to us for lots of things." (Hmm, I think I'll buy a Kubota.)

Clorox is a company that understands differentiation. When Clorox purchased Hidden Valley ranch dressing, their marketing people had the good sense not to add it to their product line and rename it Clorox Hidden Valley. In fact, the name Clorox has never appeared on any of Hidden Valley's packages, advertisements, or other marketing materials. Yet you'd be surprised at how many companies have violated common sense and paid the price. The lesson? Keep it pure, keep it different.

DRESSING, ANYONE?

IT'S DIFFERENT—I LIKE IT.

Differentiation works because of the way the human cognitive system works. Our brain acts as a filter to protect us from the vast amount of irrelevant information that surrounds us every day. To keep us from drowning in triviality, it learns to tell things apart. We get data from our senses, then compare it to data from earlier experiences, and put it into a category. Thus we can differentiate between a dog and a lion, a shadow and a crevasse, or an edible mushroom and a poisonous one (usually).

The sense we rely on mostly is sight. Our visual system is hardwired to discern the differences between the things we see, starting with the biggest differences and working down to the smallest. It looks for contrasts. It recognizes the differences between subject and ground, big and small, dark

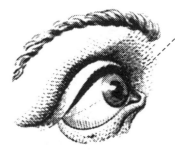

and light, rough and smooth, fat and thin, motionless and moving. Then the brain takes over and begins to make meaning. It recognizes differences such as those between near and far, old and new, light and heavy, peaceful and aggressive, simple and complex, easy and difficult.

The concerns of our visual system are related to those of aesthetics, the study of beauty. Both are about perceiving differences. What's more, the concerns of aesthetics are similar to those of branding. When we come upon a new product, package, or page layout that uses contrast masterfully—not only in its design but in its very concept—we find it aesthetically pleasing. We like it.

The traditional view of design is that it has four possible goals: to identify, to inform, to entertain, or to persuade. But with branding there's a fifth: to differentiate. While the first four are tactical, the fifth is strategic, with its roots deep in aesthetics— a powerful combination of logic and magic.

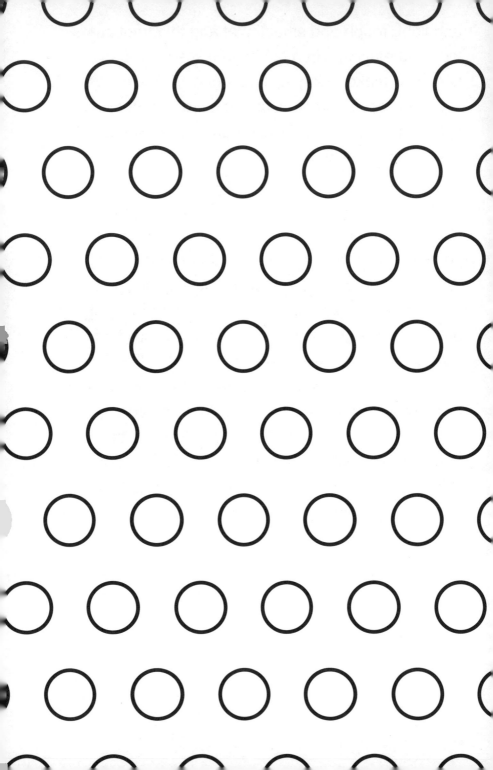

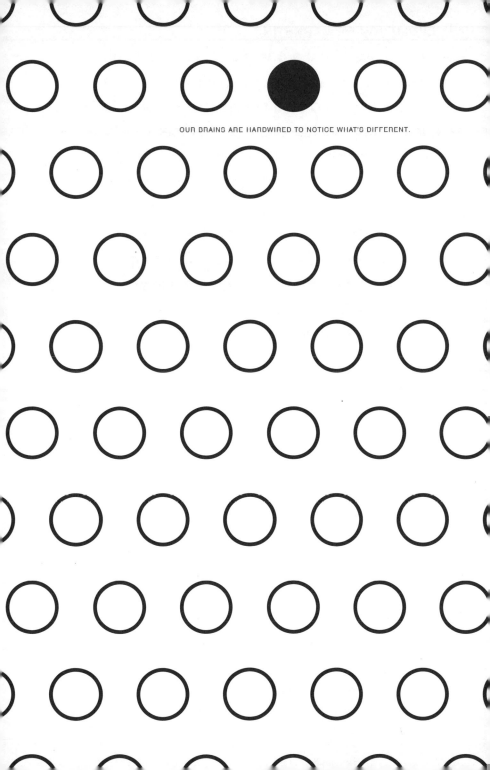

OUR BRAINS ARE HARDWIRED TO NOTICE WHAT'S DIFFERENT.

THE EVOLUTION OF MARKETING.

As we've moved from a one-size-fits-all economy to a mass-customization economy, the attention of marketing has shifted from features, to benefits, to experience, to tribal identification. In other words, selling has evolved from an emphasis on "what it has," to "what it does," to "what you'll feel," to "who you are." This shift demonstrates that, while features and benefits are still important to people, personal identity has become even more important.

Cognitive expert Edward de Bono once advised marketers that, instead of building a brand on USP (the Unique Selling Proposition of a product),

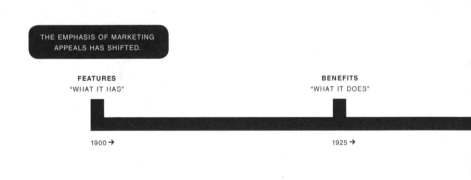

THE EMPHASIS OF MARKETING APPEALS HAS SHIFTED.

FEATURES
"WHAT IT HAS"

BENEFITS
"WHAT IT DOES"

1900 →

1925 →

DIFFERENTIATE

they should pay more attention to "UBS" (the Unique Buying State of their customers). He was ahead of his time in predicting the rise of consumer-centric marketing.

The success of the Nike brand is ample proof that de Bono's concept works. As a weekend athlete, my two nagging doubts are that I might be congenitally lazy, and that I might have little actual ability. I'm not really worried about my shoes. But when the Nike folks say, "Just do it," they're peering into my soul. I begin to feel that, if they understand me that well, their shoes are probably pretty good. I'm then willing to join the tribe of Nike.

EXPERIENCE
"WHAT YOU'LL FEEL"

IDENTIFICATION
"WHO YOU ARE"

1950 →

2000 →

GLOBALISM VS. TRIBALISM.

We've heard a lot of talk about globalism—the knocking down of national, economic, and cultural barriers to create a single society. In the 1960s Marshall McLuhan envisioned a world so connected by technology that the old divisions would disappear, made obsolete by a massive "global village." Forty years later we have no global village, and we probably never will, at least in the usual sense of a village—an intimate community united by a single language and culture. Instead we have a global communication network, an electronic layer on top of the old divisions that influences them and adds to them, but doesn't replace them.

The fact is, we need divisions just as much as we need ways to transcend them. Without barriers there would be no safety—against war, disease, natural disaster, a feeling of alienation, of being lost in an uncaring world. The faster globalism removes barriers, the faster people erect new ones. They create intimate worlds they can understand, and where they can be somebody and feel as if they belong. They create tribes.

If you stretch the concept of tribe just a little, you can see that a brand creates a kind of tribe.

Depending on your Unique Buying State, you can join any number of tribes on any number of days and feel part of something bigger than yourself. You can belong to the Callaway tribe when you play golf, the VW tribe when you drive to work, and the Williams-Sonoma tribe when you cook a meal. You're part of a select clan (or so you feel) when you buy products from these clearly differentiated companies. Brands are the little gods of modern life, each ruling a different need, activity, mood, or situation. Yet you're in control. If your latest god falls from Olympus, you can switch to another one.

ON SUNDAYS THEY WORSHIP HARLEY, GOD OF THE OPEN ROAD.

DIFFERENTIATE

IS THIS HOW YOUR

CUSTOMERS SEE YOU?

FOCUS, FOCUS, FOCUS.

These are the three most important words in branding. The danger is rarely too much focus, but too little. An unfocused brand is one that's so broad that it doesn't stand for anything. A focused brand, by contrast, knows exactly what it is, why it's different, and why people want it.

Yet focus is difficult to achieve because it means giving something up. It runs counter to our most basic marketing instinct: If we narrow our offering, won't we narrow our opportunities for profit? Answer: Not necessarily. It's often better to be number one in a small category than to be number three in a large one. At number three your strategy may have to include a low price, whereas at number one you can charge a premium. History has shown that it pays handsomely to be number one in your category—first, because of higher margins, and second, because the risk of com-moditization is almost nonexistent. Yet number two can also be profitable, despite a smaller market share. Number three, or four, or five, however, may only be worth the effort if you think you have a realistic shot at becoming number two someday.

Can't be number one or number two? Redefine your category. The industrial-strength software product Framemaker only made it to number three as a word-processing product, but as a document-publishing product it quickly became number one, with double its previous sales. All it took was a change of focus.

Competition forces specialization. The law of the jungle is "survival of the fittingest," and the smart company doesn't wait to be forced. In the competitive world of automobiles, for example, Volvo built a bulletproof brand when it turned a heavy, boxy vehicle into the "safe" alternative, a market niche they were able to own and defend for many years. Was that good enough for Volvo? Apparently not, because they've recently added fast, sexy vehicles to their lineup. Time will tell if the concept of raciness is compatible with the concept of safety. In trying to satisfy every desire, Volvo may be weaving recklessly down the road toward no man's brand.

Brand guru David Aaker likens growing a brand to managing a timber reserve: You plant new trees for future profit and you harvest old trees for profits today. The trick with brand is to know which is which. What may seem like growing a brand may actually be harvesting it. Take line extensions. When you have a successful product or service, a nearly irresistible temptation is to "leverage" the brand, to extend it into a family. It makes complete sense— except when it doesn't.

Brand extensions make sense when new additions to the family serve to strengthen the meaning of the brand, adding mass and definition to whatever it is that makes it different. In the supermarket, a good example of growth by brand extension is Oxo Good Grips, the clever line of hand tools whose every new addition reinforces its ownership of the easy-grip/high-style/black-and-white-pack category.

Brand extensions make less sense when they're driven by a desire for short-term profits without regard to focus. What makes them especially seductive is that they can work remarkably well in the short term, even as they undermine the position of the brand. A recent example of defocusing by brand extension is the Cayenne, an SUV from Porsche. In a single misguided stroke, Porsche has pulled the rug out from under its reputation as a maker of classic sports cars. They maintain that the Cayenne is an example of Porsche innovation, but Porsche fans will say it's a grab for profits in a tired market. Had Porsche invented the SUV, people might see it as innovation, but at the tail-end of the trend it looks more like greed—especially since Porsche is already highly profitable. Naturally, the new car will sell. It's got the revered Porsche styling, engineering, and pedigree, all of which can be harvested through line extension. But the question is, what does Porsche now stand for?

Even in the best of times, the principle of focus is a hard mistress, demanding fidelity, courage, and determination. And when a company faces additional pressure from stockholder expectations, political infighting, unexpected competition, or changes in management, there's a temptation to extend the product line for short-term relief, even at the expense of its market position. Resist, because the long-term survival of a brand depends on staying focused. As positioning expert Jack Trout succinctly puts it, "differentiate or die."

BY STAYING FOCUSED, THE GOOD GRIPS BRAND HAS GROWN STRONGER WITH EVERY BRAND EXTENSION.

DISCIPLINE 2 : COLLABORATE

IT TAKES A VILLAGE TO BUILD A BRAND.

In her book, THE NATURE OF ECONOMIES, Jane Jacobs writes that economic development is not just expansion, but differentiation emerging from generality, much like evolutionary or embryological development in nature. Moreover, she says, differentiation depends on codevelopment—no entity, natural or economic, evolves in isolation.

Brands don't develop in isolation, either. They result from the interaction of thousands of people over a long period of time. Branding requires not only the work of executives and marketing people who manage the brand, but an ever-changing roster of strategy consultants, design firms, advertising agencies, research companies, PR firms, industrial designers, environmental designers, and so on. It also requires the valuable contributions of employees, suppliers, distributors, partners, stockholders, and customers—an entire branding community. It takes a village to build a brand.

Building a brand today is a little like building a cathedral during the Renaissance. It took hundreds of craftsmen scores of years, even generations, to complete a major edifice. Each craftsman added his own piece to the project—a carving, a window, a fresco, a dome—always keeping an eye on the total effect. Like yesterday's cathedrals, many of today's brands are too large and too complex to be managed by one person or one department. They require teams of specialists, sharing ideas and coordinating the efforts across a creative network.

Management guru Peter Drucker maintains that the most important shift in business today is from "ownership" to "partnership," and from "individual tasks" to "collaboration." The successful company is not the one with the most brains, he suggests, but the most brains acting in concert. Brand managers and communication firms are responding to this new challenge in a number of interesting ways.

LIKE BUILDING
A CATHEDRAL,
BUILDING A BRAND
IS A COLLABORATIVE
EFFORT.

THE NEW COLLABORATIVES.

Today there are three basic models for managing brand collaboration: 1) outsourcing the brand to a one-stop shop, 2) outsourcing it to a brand agency, and 3) stewarding the brand internally with an integrated marketing team. All three models are forward-thinking responses to the problem, because they recognize brand as a network activity. Let's examine them one at a time.

The first model, the one-stop shop, has its roots in early 20th-century branding, when companies routinely consigned large portions of their communications to a single firm, typically an advertising agency. The advertising agency would conduct research, develop strategy, create campaigns, and measure the results. The main benefit was efficiency, since one person within the client company could direct the entire brand effort. As branding has grown more complex, so has the one-stop shop. Today's one-stop is either a single multi-disciplinary firm, or a holding company with a collection of

COMPANY

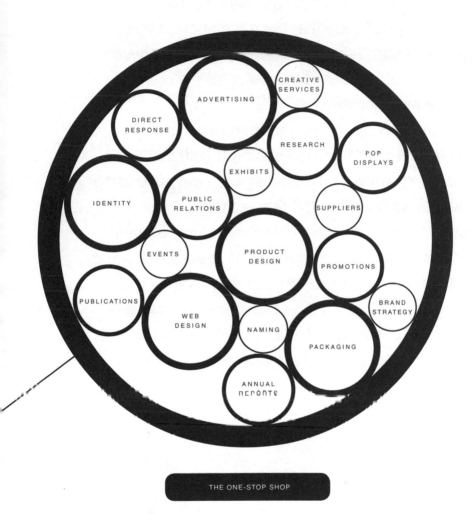

CREATIVE
SERVICES

ADVERTISING

DIRECT
RESPONSE

RESEARCH

POP
DISPLAYS

EXHIBITS

IDENTITY

PUBLIC
RELATIONS

SUPPLIERS

EVENTS

PRODUCT
DESIGN

PROMOTIONS

PUBLICATIONS

WEB
DESIGN

NAMING

BRAND
STRATEGY

PACKAGING

ANNUAL
REPORTS

THE ONE-STOP SHOP

specialist firms. The advantages of the one-stop shop are an ability to unify a message across media, and ease of management for the client. The drawbacks are that the various disciplines are not usually the best of breed, and, in effect, the company cedes stewardship of the brand to the one-stop shop.

The second model, the brand agency, is a variation of the one-stop concept. With this model the client works with a lead agency (an advertising agency, design firm, PR firm, strategy firm, or other brand firm), which helps assemble a team of specialist firms to work on the brand. The brand agency leads the project, and may even act as a contractor, paying the other firms as subcontractors. The advantages of this model are the ability to unify a message across media, and the freedom to work with best-of-breed specialists. A drawback is that stewardship of the brand still resides more with the brand agency than with the client company.

COMPANY

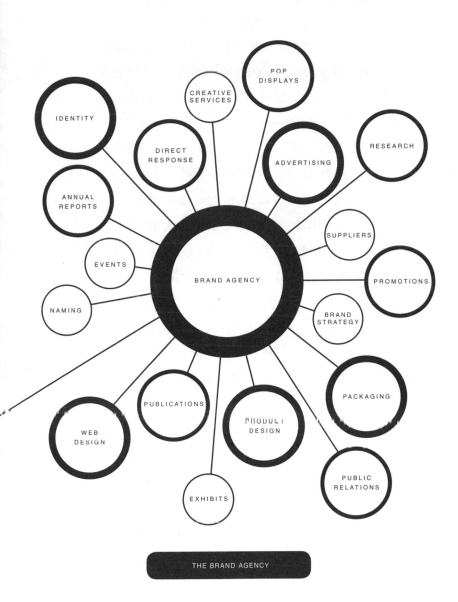

POP
DISPLAYS

CREATIVE
SERVICES

IDENTITY

DIRECT
RESPONSE

ADVERTISING

RESEARCH

ANNUAL
REPORTS

SUPPLIERS

EVENTS

BRAND AGENCY

PROMOTIONS

NAMING

BRAND
STRATEGY

PUBLICATIONS

PACKAGING

WEB
DESIGN

PRODUCT
DESIGN

PUBLIC
RELATIONS

EXHIBITS

THE BRAND AGENCY

The third model, the integrated marketing team, bears little resemblance to the traditional out-sourcing model. It sees branding as a continuous network activity that needs to be controlled from within the company. In this model, best-of-breed specialist firms are selected to work alongside internal marketing people on a virtual "superteam," which is then "coached" by the company's design manager. The advantages of this model are the ability to unify a message across media, the freedom to work with best-of-breed specialists, plus internal stewardship. This last benefit is important, because it means that brand knowledge can accrue to the company, instead of vanishing through a revolving door with the last firm to work on it. A drawback of an inte-grated marketing team is that it requires a strong internal team to run it.

Of course, while these three types of collabo-ratives seem tidy in print, they're messier in practice. Companies are mixing and matching aspects of all three models as they grope their way to a new collaborative paradigm. Still others are behind the curve, unaware that there's a revolution afoot.

ANNUAL REPORTS

EVENTS

EXHIBITS

PUBLIC RELATIONS

WEB DESIGN

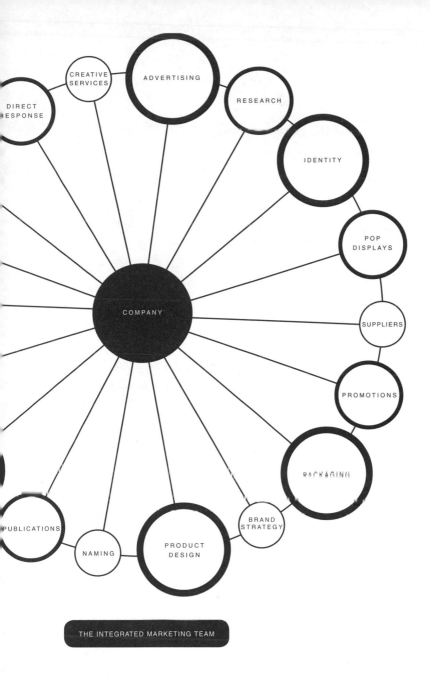

CREATIVE SERVICES

ADVERTISING

RESEARCH

DIRECT RESPONSE

IDENTITY

POP DISPLAYS

COMPANY

SUPPLIERS

PROMOTIONS

PACKAGING

PUBLICATIONS

NAMING

PRODUCT DESIGN

BRAND STRATEGY

THE INTEGRATED MARKETING TEAM

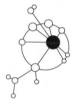

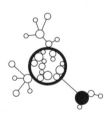

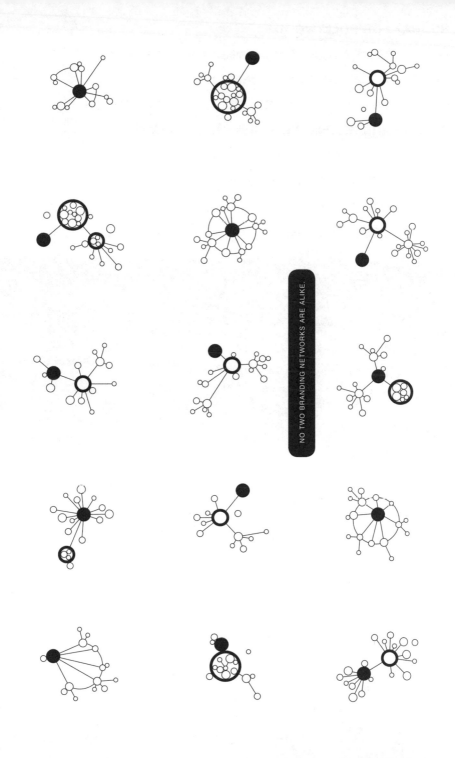

NO TWO BRANDING NETWORKS ARE ALIKE.

HOORAY FOR HOLLYWOOD.

According to a recent McKinsey report, the next economy will see a significant rise in network organizations—groups of "unbundled" companies cooperating across the value chain to deliver products and services to customers. By owning fewer assets and leveraging the resources of partner companies, these network orchestrators require less capital, return higher revenues per

employee, and spread the risks of a volatile market across the network.

The network organization isn't new; a successful model of unbundling has existed for years. It's called Hollywood.

A half-century ago, the major Hollywood studios not only owned the soundstages and backlots necessary for their movies, but also the producers, directors, writers, actors, cinematographers, musicians, PR specialists, and distributors. Some even built theater chains for the exclusive use of their own properties. As the dream machines cranked out hundreds of look-alike movies to feed their growing overhead, movie-making began to slide from craft

to commodity. The independents soon learned how to end-run the mega-studios by producing high-quality "little" films and low-budget B-movies.

What happened next? The big studios learned from the small ones, and began unbundling their vertically integrated companies. By switching to a network model, the studios could avail themselves of the best talent for each project, thereby creating unique products and shedding unnecessary overhead. In reversing the trend toward commoditization, they encouraged the growth of an artisan community, not unlike those

that grew up around the cathedrals of Europe. Like the cathedral-builders, Hollywood specialists don't see themselves as technicians, but as craftspeople working in a creative network.

Hollywood isn't unique, just more evolved than other industries. In the 1980s, Silicon Valley faced a similar challenge when Japan threatened to walk away with its franchise in microchips, duplicating their features and undercutting prices. Valley companies quickly discovered the value of open collaboration, producing ever-more-advanced systems and components that kept them one step ahead of the copycats.

In the mid-1990s I was privileged to be a member of the superteam that launched Netscape Navigator, along with related products and services.

Production Secretary — MISS ALBERS
Hong Kong Kung Fu Coordinator — CECIL LEM
Assistant to Esteban Diaz — FREDA HILEBURN
Assistant to Julia Padar — CECILY FREED
Assistant to Lawrence Canell — LEE SKIDMORE
Assistant to Billie Jo Kramer — MICHAEL SCHER
Assistant to Raul Bellagio — CARMEN TRUAND
Assistant to Lisa Maitland — ROGER FENESTRAID
Assistant to Stephen Skye — CARLA JONES
Assistant to Joel Dartmouth — BELLA REINGOLD
Assistant to Kelly Marin — OWEN FLAGG
American Casting — CHARLA HEMINGWAY
Extras Casting — ALICE TRAUN
Dialect Coach — MARINA GREYSTONE
Physical Trainers — CHUCK BENNIS
Sports Masseuse — MANDY GLADDINGS
Medical Advisors — DR. KEVIN BLASKET
DR. ROBERT KLEINMAN
HELEN ROBERTS
Publicist — KATHERINE TOPEK
Safety Coordinator — STEVEN HODGKINS
Safety Officers — DARREL PROVIDA
JENNIFER LANG
BENTON GAI
Nurse — JAMES HOWARD
Unit Manager — COREEN RICHARDSON
Assistant Unit Manager — DELBA CONNORS
Construction Supervisor — JACK LAMBERT
Construction Coordinator — CAROL TREFETHEN
Scenic Artist — JOEL PICKERING
Construction — NED B. MACKENAW
GREGOR STANDVICH
MIKE PEAL
DENNIS STIVEY
PETER CASTERINI
JIM BORDEN
STUBBY FREY
MACK VENABLE
CLIVE BARNSWALLOW
BILL DIEUX
MILLI PEDERSEN
SYLVIA TOM
MICHEL S. MAISTRE
CARLY MAHONEY
Caterers

2nd Unit
Director — BENJAMIN HAWKS
Director of Photography — PAUL MINTER
1st Assistant Director — DEXTER LLOYD
Production Coordinators — JOSH KETTERING
SHARON DAY
HANNAH SUNCH
1st Assistant Camera — BUCKY BURNSIDE
Gaffer — TIM O'RILEY
Best Boy — HANK MAZURKI
Key Grip — BRIAN DREBB
Dolly Grip — KEITH YAMAZAKI
Script Supervisor — MAUREEN AIGLE
Video Operator — HELMUT DRESCH
Locations Manager — BOB TAUBIN
Props — TINA GRENOBLE
JO BANNISTER
Make-up Artist — JENNIFER DREYFUS
Wardrobe — CORNELIA POND
Unit Manager — ANDY KADEL
Assistant Unit Manager — STEPHEN B. GOODE

My firm developed the Navigator icon and the retail package, while other firms, including an advertising agency, a web design firm, a PR group, and an exhibit design firm, worked on their own pieces to help launch the product at warp speed. This example of "parallel processing" showed how collaboration can yield not only quality but quickness.

Netscape was formed in 1994, went public in 1995, and was absorbed into AOL by 1999. During this short period, it launched more than a dozen products and changed the direction of computing.

Thanks to the Hollywood model, design managers are now learning how to assemble top-notch teams of specialists, inspire them to work together productively—even joyfully—then disband them when the project's over, only to reassemble them

Caterers ANNE MARIE DONALD NANCY SIMS KATIE VALERIO LINDA STAVROS BECKY TINE CAROLINE DEVERE

Staff Assistants BARBARA BOSTON MARGARET CHU CARMEN STEVENSON DEB FARGO JESSICA BELVEDERE MARGE FREY ANN MILLAIRE CECELIA LADBROKE DENNIE CHAN PATRICIA BALLARD T. K. MALONE RENALDA KLINE MATTIE BOK KEITH BRELLIG LANA KARLSON STACY AMBORGRAST MARIA GARCIA JEFF GIMBEL

Visual Effects Producer

ANIMAL INSTINCTS, LLC
Handler-in-Chief MASON KIMBALL
Assistant Handler MARIAN DWYER
Snake Wrangler TONY MAGGIORE
Trainers KELLIE PATRICK DON DELILIO SUE FRAMPTON
Veterinary Advisor DR. JANICE CRUMB

EFFEX VISUALE, LLC
Assoc SFX Supv MARTHA KLEMENT
Technology Supv SVEN PERLING
Asst Digital Coord KATRINA MOLINARI
Color and Lighting CANDIE CANE BARRY K. LATHAM ADRIAN TAROOD JOHN STILL
Systems Manager IVAN DEVESTER
Systems Admin STEVEN KELLOGG
Systems Support ANGELO FORI
Character Animators GASTON LAPTER
Compositors KERRY DEAS DAVE SHELTON KIM FORTES BREIARD MASORR GENEVIEVE MASSEAU DENISE TRENT
Digital FX Producer JOCK ORR
Digital FX Supv RICHARD FOXEN
Digital Line Producer MAIRE CONNELY
Production Aide XAVIER LANDT
FX Aide/Asst CANDICE FREER
Software Developer MAXWELL GORMON

SFX Producer UPTON BORDERS
Line Producer KATHY HOWARTH
Scene Office JOSIE NEUWIRTH
Lead Tech Supv TONY BAGHETTI
Asst Tech Supv JASON SAGMEISTER
Texture Painter ARTHUR WOO CHRISTOPHER HYDE
2D/3D Paint JANTA KHAN
Matte Painting CHRISTA JACKET
Lead Scene Painter BRAD TOMKINS
Computer Paint AKIO YAMADA
FX Animator BERENICE MORLO
2D Texture Painter STAN WEBER
2D Point Asst BONNIE CREAM
Conceptual Art MARGERY LENNON LISA DARMA
Editors KELLIE GRETSCH MANDIE BRIGG HUBERT MALLE JASON FLAGGOT MARK HALFRIDGE STEVE SCOTT DELBART MINOR

Film Recordist
Prop Builders
Technical Support

ART ATTACK, INC.
Technical Supv GRETCHEN OLIN
Tech Consultant DUSTIN BIRKAT
Camera PATRICK MENGES
2D Animator CECIL STINE

in a different configuration for the next project. The lesson hasn't been lost on other industries. Soon every knowledge-based business will adopt some version of the Hollywood model, and, years from now, many will undoubtedly agree with Noel Coward's statement that "work was more fun than fun."

THE NETSCAPE BRAND
WAS BUILT ON THE
HOLLYWOOD MODEL.

COLLABORATE

THE POWER OF PROTOTYPES.

Not all Hollywood movies are hits, but very few are bombs. They're usually saved from that ignominious fate by the use of prototypes—scripts and story-boards. The script is the prototype for the story, and the storyboard is the prototype for production. Any major problems with the movie can be corrected at the prototype stage, long before much money is spent. The script and the storyboard, once approved, keep all the collaborators on track, from the director to the continuity person.

Branding projects use prototypes as well. Instead of a script, brand collaborators rely on a creative brief; instead of a storyboard, they use mockups or drafts. What makes prototypes so powerful, to borrow a phrase from Tom Kelley of the industrial design firm IDEO, is that they provide a "near life" experience for the collaborators. Everyone on the team, from the brand manager to the design intern, can immediately sense whether the concept will work in the real world. No amount of talking or arm-waving can accomplish this feat as well as prototypes.

Prototypes can also cut through the "red tape" of marketing documents. Instead of starting with a list of features and working toward a concept, team members can go straight to a concept, then add whatever features are needed to support it. And if the concept looks like a loser? Hey—it's just a concept—start over with a new one. Since a brand is a person's gut feeling about a product, service, or company, gut feeling is the fastest way to get there. Prototypes create a playground for collaborative ideas, allowing ample space for the right side of the brain to work its magic.

=11

THE MATHEMATICS
OF COLLABORATION IS
NOTHING LESS THAN MAGIC.

DISCIPLINE 3 : INNOVATE

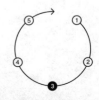

WHERE THE RUBBER MEETS THE ROAD.

A combination of good strategy and poor execution is like a Ferrari with flat tires. It looks good in the specs, but fails on the street. This is the case for at least half the brand communication done today. Don't take my word for it—pick up a copy of your favorite magazine and leaf through the ads. How many actually touch your emotions? Will you remember any of them tomorrow? If not, it's probably the fault of execution, not strategy. Execution—read creativity—is the most difficult part of the branding mix to control. It's magic, not logic, that ignites passion in customers.

Our cultural distrust in creativity goes back to the Enlightenment, when we discovered the awesome power of rational thinking. The movement became so successful that rational thinking became the only thinking—at least the only thinking you could trust. Yet in spite of our continuing reverence for rationality, we don't really do many things by logic. Our best thinking depends more on the "illogical" skills of intuition and insight, which may explain why logical argument rarely convinces anyone of anything important.

Benjamin Franklin, despite being a child of the Enlightenment, showed both intuition and insight when he observed: "Would you persuade, speak of interest, not of reason."

Innovation requires creativity, and creativity gives many business people a twitch. Anything new, by definition, is untried, and therefore unsafe. Yet when you ask executives where they expect to find their most sustainable competitive advantage, what do they answer? Innovation. Because the truth is, innovation lies at the heart of both better design and better business. It magnifies drive inside the organization. It slashes the costs of inefficiency, duplication, and corporate ennui. It confers the ability to produce uncommon, yet practical, responses to real problems.

INNOVATION IS WHAT GIVES BRANDS
TRACTION IN THE MARKETPLACE.

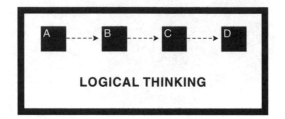

LOGICAL THINKING

WHEN EVERYBODY ZIGS, ZAG.

Would-be leaders in any industry must come to
grips with a self-evident truth—you can't be a leader
by following. Admittedly, it's difficult to zag when
every bone in your body says zig. Human beings
are social animals—our natural inclination is to go
with the group.

  Creativity, however, demands the opposite.
It requires an unnatural act. To achieve originality
we need to abandon the comforts of habit, reason,
and the approval of our peers, and strike out in
new directions. In the world of branding, creativity
doesn't require reinventing the wheel, but simply
thinking in fresh ways. It requires looking for
what industrial designer Raymond Loewy called

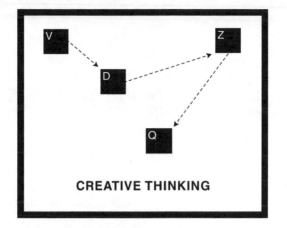

CREATIVE THINKING

MAYA—the Most Advanced Yet Acceptable solution. Creative professionals excel at MAYA. While market researchers describe how the world is, creative people describe how it could be. Their thinking is often so fresh that they zag even when they should zig. But without fresh thinking, there's no chance of magic.

An effective use of the MAYA principle was the career of The Beatles. They began in the early 1960s with songs that were commonly acceptable, then raised the bar of innovation one record at a time. By the end of the decade, they had taken their audience on a wild ride from the commonplace to the sublime, and in the process created the anthems for a cultural revolution. Their formula? As one critic observed: "They never did the same thing once."

AUDIENCES WANT MORE THAN LOGIC.

BRAND OR BLAND?

Q: How do you know when an idea is innovative?

A: When it scares the hell out of everybody.

A friend of mine once observed that the only thing worse than the fear of death is the "fear of stupid." Some companies are so afraid of appearing less than dignified that they settle for proud, stiff, or inhuman. Against this backdrop of stuffed shirts, smart companies have an excellent chance to stand out—to zag. The Volkswagen Bug did it to great effect in the 1960s (and again in the 1990s) by using self-deprecating humor as a strategic weapon. But humor is only one way to surprise people. Mostly it just takes the guts to be different.

Of course, while audiences may reward guts, corporations usually don't. Japanese salarymen have a saying: "The nail that sticks up gets hammered down." Corporate America has a similar saying: "Don't rock the boat." No wonder people are afraid of signing off on new ideas—by keeping your head down you're more likely to keep it attached. Then where will innovation come from? Most likely from the outside, or from people inside who think outside.

THE NAIL THAT STICKS UP
IS ONE BRAVE NAIL.

THOSE CRAZY NEW NAMES.

Agilent, Agilis, Ajilon, and Agere. Advantix, Advantis, Adventis, and Advanta. Actuant, Equant, Guidant, and Reliant. Prodigy, Certegy, Centegy, and Tality. Why are there so many sound-alike names? The short answer is this: Most of the good names are taken. Between a rising tide of startups on one hand, and a flood of URLs on the other, companies are continually forced to dive deeper for workable names. The latest trend is to push the boundaries of dignity with names like Yahoo!, Google, FatSplash, and Jamcracker. Where will it end?

It won't. The need for good brand names origi-nates with customers, and customers will always want convenient ways of identifying, remembering, discussing, and comparing brands. The right name can be a brand's most valuable asset, driving differ-entiation and speeding acceptance. The wrong name can cost millions, even billions, in workarounds and lost income over the lifetime of the brand. George Bernard Shaw's advice applies to brands as well as people: "Take care to get born well."

Of course, some names haven't been created so much as inherited. A good example of a heritage name is Smuckers, which marketing people have often cited as a bad name with a clever spin. "With a name like Smuckers, it has to be good," goes the well-known slogan. But Smuckers was a good name from day one—distinctive, short, spellable, pronounceable, likable, portable, and protectable. And while the company presents it as slightly silly, the name benefits strongly from onomatopoeia. "Smuckers" sounds like smacking lips, the pre-verbal testament to a yummy jam.

"WITH A NAME LIKE SMUCKERS,
IT **BETTER** BE GOOD."
—RED SKELTON

Another heritage name is Carl Zeiss, the maker of optical lenses. Does Zeiss make great lenses? Who knows? But the name makes the lenses "sound" great. The word "Zeiss" has hints of "glass" and "precise," and evokes thoughts of German technological superiority. The name works so well that it can stretch to include high-end sunglasses and other precision products without the risk of breakage.

Generally speaking, high-imagery names are more memorable than low-imagery names. Names constructed from Greek and Latin root words tend to be low-imagery names. Accenture and Innoveda come to mind. Names that use Anglo-Saxon words, or the names of people, tend to be high-imagery names, producing vivid mental pictures that aid recall. Think of Apple Computer and Betty Crocker. Some of most powerful names are those that combine well with a visual treatment to create a memorable brand icon.

THE 7 CRITERIA FOR A GOOD NAME:

1. **DISTINCTIVENESS.** Does it stand out from the crowd, especially from other names in its class? Does it separate well from ordinary text and speech? The best brand names have the "presence" of a proper noun.

2. **BREVITY.** Is it short enough to be easily recalled and used? Will it resist being reduced to a nickname? Long multi-word names will be quickly shortened to non-communicating initials.

3. **APPROPRIATENESS.** Is there a reasonable fit with the business purpose of the entity? If it would work just as well—or better—for another entity, keep looking.

4. **EASY SPELLING AND PRONUNCIATION.** Will most people be able to spell the name after hearing it spoken? Will they be able to pronounce it after seeing it written? A name shouldn't turn into a spelling test or make people feel ignorant.

5. **LIKABILITY.** Will people enjoy using it? Names that are intellectually stimulating, or provide a good "mouth feel," have a headstart over those that don't.

6. **EXTENDIBILITY.** Does it have "legs"? Does it suggest a visual interpretation or lend itself to a number of creative executions? Great names provide endless opportunities for brandplay.

7. **PROTECTABILITY.** Can it be trademarked? Is it available for web use? While many names can be trademarked, some names are more defensible than others, making them safer and more valuable in the long run.

AVATARS RUN CIRCLES
AROUND LOGOS.

ICONS AND AVATARS.

A brand icon is a name and visual symbol that communicate a market position. An avatar is an icon that can move, morph, or otherwise operate freely as the brand's alter ego. For icon, think Shell; for avatar, think Cingular. Icons can sometimes be upgraded to avatars, as AT&T has done by animating its striped globe icon in its TV spots.

Logos are dead! Long live icons and avatars! Why? Because logos as we know them—logotypes, monograms, abstract symbols, and other two-dimensional trademarks—are products of the printing press and mass communication. They evolved as a way to identify brands rather than to differentiate them. Today marketers realize that branding is not about stamping a trademark on anything that moves. It's about managing relationships between the company and its constituents, conducting a conversation among many people over many channels. We still have the printing press at our beck and call, but we also have the Internet, TV, telemarketing, live events, and other media to work with. Icons and avatars respond to this new reality by jumping off the printed page and interacting with people wherever they are.

Aristotle was a born brander. He believed that "perception starts with the eye," and that "the greatest thing by far is to be a master of metaphor."

These two principles create the basis of brand icons. Cognitive scientists estimate that more than half the brain is dedicated to the visual system, adding weight to the argument that a trademark should be strongly visual. Yet it can also involve other senses, including smell, touch, taste, or hearing. Take for example, the auditory counterpart to an icon, sometimes called an "earcon." The experience of flying United Airlines is now inextricably linked to Gershwin's "Rhapsody in Blue," and the Intel Inside brand would be less memorable without its "bong" sound bite.

When conceived well, an icon is a repository of meaning. It contains the DNA of the brand, the basic material for creating a total personality distinct

WHO CAN HEAR RHAPSODY IN BLUE WITHOUT THINKING OF UNITED?

INNOVATE

from the competition. The meanings that are packed into the icon can be unpacked at will and woven into all the brand communications, from advertising to signage, from web pages to trade show booths, from packaging to the products themselves. An avatar goes even further by becoming the symbolic actor in a continuing brand story. As trademarks go from two dimensions to three and four dimensions, the old-style logo may begin to seem more like a tintype than a motion picture.

IT'S ALL PACKAGING.

While not all brands are products and not all products are sold at retail, a book on brand would be remiss to ignore the importance of packaging. For many products, the package is the branding. It's also the last and best chance to influence a prospect this side of the checkout counter.

In some retail environments, such as the supermarket, it's possible for a package to reach 100% of people shopping in that category. For several seconds, or even a few precious minutes, the shopper is completely focused on the differences among brands. Previous intentions to buy one product over another are suddenly put aside and memories of past advertising are shoved into the background as the competing packages go "mano a mano" for the shopper's attention. This is known as a branding moment.

Retail brand managers funnel a large portion of their marketing budgets into package design, because the return on investment is likely to be higher with packaging than with advertising, promotion, public relations, or other spending options. For many retail products, packaging not only makes the final sale, it strikes a significant blow for the brand, since experience with the product is often the best foundation for customer loyalty.

Marketers know this, but they're not sure what makes it work. How, exactly, does one package beat another at the point of sale? How much of the battle is won by logic and how much by magic? Is it science or art? As you might guess, it's both. But since most marketers favor left-brain thinking, most packages end up heavy on facts and light on emotion, the ingredient customers want most. Instead, customers are greeted with features, benefits, and what one shopper I interviewed called "scientific mumbo jumbo."

Before you can create emotion with a package, however, you need to understand the natural reading sequence of your category. It so happens that customers process messages in a certain order, depending on the product, and messages presented out of order go unheeded.

Here's an example of a typical reading sequence: 1) the shopper notices the package on the shelf— the result of good colors, strong contrast, an arresting

A RETAIL PACKAGE IS THE LAST AND BEST CHANCE TO MAKE A SALE.

photo, bold typography, or other technique; 2) the shopper mentally asks "What is it?," bringing the product name and category into play; 3) then "Why should I care?," which is best answered with a very brief why-to-buy message; 4) which in turn elicits a desire for more information to define and support the why-to-buy message; 5) the shopper is finally ready for the "mumbo-jumbo" necessary to make a decision—features, price, compatibilities, guarantees, awards, or whatever the category dictates.

When you present these pieces of information in a natural reading sequence, you increase their resonance and create a sympathetic bond with the customer. But if you lead off with features when the customer simply wants to know why she should care, the message that may come through is this: "Our product's features are more important than your interests." Advertising pioneer David Ogilvy often claimed that by changing a single word in a headline one could increase effectiveness of an

advertisement by up to ten times. In my own practice, I've proven (at least to myself) that by getting
the reading sequence right, and by connecting
product features to customer emotions, a package
can increase product sales by up to three times,
sometimes more.

But what if you don't sell at retail? No matter.
The principles used in successful packaging—
clarity, emotion, and a natural reading sequence—
apply to every type of brand design. When you think
about it, branding is simply a convenient package
for a business idea.

DOES OUR WEBSITE LOOK FAT IN THIS DRESS?

The award for Most Egregious Disregard of Natural Reading Sequence goes to…that's right, the World Wide Web. Arguably the most promising medium of our time, the web took off like a rocket, but failed to escape the dense atmosphere of its own hype. That's because the web, while a technical achievement, has been a usability nightmare. It began as the brainchild of a colony of feature-loving geeks, who fed it capability after capability until it became a hydra-head of non-information.

Most of today's home pages ignore the basic

WHICH SITE LOOKS

rules of visual aesthetics, including contrast, legi-
bility, pacing, and reading sequence. Uncultivated
websites shove a tangle of unruly data in your face,
then expect you to sort it out: a typical home page
tries to squeeze an average of 25 pieces of information, some of it animated, into an area the size
of a handkerchief. The closest relative of today's
web page is a newspaper page, yet most home
pages make newspaper pages seem easy to navi-
gate. The concept of a natural reading sequence
has yet to reach the bastion of bad taste we
fondly call the web.

EASIER TO USE?

Netscape: Google

Google™

| Web | Images | Groups | Directory |

- Advanced Search
- Preferences
- Language Tools

[Google Search] [I'm Feeling Lucky]

New! Get the Google Search Appliance for your corporation.

Search or read your favorite catalogs using Google.

Advertise with Us - Search Solutions - News and Resources - Jobs, Press, Cool Stuff...

©2002 Google - Searching 2,073,418,204 web pages

Okay, let's be fair. The designers of newspapers, books, movies, and television have had more time to refine their aesthetic "best practices." Television shows were pretty hokey until the networks became big business and competition forced the issue. But what exactly are the invisible chains keeping web design from achieving its full potential? It boils down to three: technophobia, turfismo, and featuritis.

TECHNOPHOBIA, the fear of new technology, keeps a lot of skilled designers out of web design. They're mostly afraid the technical demands of the medium will engulf their projects, leaving little time to work on the aesthetics. The result is that most web design, thus deprived of disciplined design-ers, still falls below the aesthetic level considered standard for catalogs, annual reports, and books.

TURFISMO, the second problem, is the behind-the-screen politicking that transforms the home page into a patchwork of tiny fiefdoms. You can see exactly which departments have the power and which don't, as turfy managers fight for space on the company marquee. Simplify the home page? Sure, but not at my expense!

Finally, FEATURITIS, an infectious desire for MORE, afflicts everyone from the CEO to the programmer. The tendency to add features, articles, graphics, animations, links, buttons, bells, and whistles comes naturally to most people. The ability to subtract features is the rare gift of the true communicator. An oft-heard excuse for cluttered pages is that most people hate clicking, and prefer to see all their choices on one page. The truth is, most people LIKE clicking—they just hate waiting. Eternal waiting, along with confusion and clutter, are the real enemies of communication. Put your website on a diet. You'll find that subtraction, not addition, is the formula for clear communication.

All brand innovation, whether for a website, a package, a product, an event, or an ad campaign, should be aimed at creating a positive experience for the user. The trick is in knowing which experience will be the MOST positive—even before you commit to it.

DISCIPLINE 4 : VALIDATE

THE NEW COMMUNICATION MODEL.

The standard model for communication has three components: sender, message, and receiver. The sender (your company) develops a message (web page, ad, brochure, direct mail piece, etc.) and sends it to a receiver (your target audience). Communication complete.

What this model fails to recognize is that real-world communication is a dialog. I say something to you, you say something back. You may say it only to yourself, like when you read a magazine ad, but your brain is nevertheless an indispensible component of the total communication system. You respond by buying the advertised brand, or by mentally storing the information for future use, or by simply turning the page. With the standard communication model, the sender doesn't know— and seemingly doesn't care—how the receiver actually responded.

OLD COMMUNICATION MODEL

The standard model is an antique. Today we can no longer afford to close our eyes, catapult a message into the ether, cross our fingers, and hope that it hits the target. Companies need feedback. Feedback turns communication into something more like a theatre performance than a magazine. If we're dying on stage, the audience lets us know. The feedback is immediate and unambiguous, which lets us make appropriate changes before the next performance.

NEW COMMUNICATION MODEL

When we solicit feedback from customers, the communication model has a fourth component. The sender creates a message, sends it to a receiver, and, instead of stopping there, the communication continues as the receiver sends a message back. With every turn around the feedback loop, the communication gets stronger and more focused. The new model is a blueprint for revolution. It transforms marketing communication into a contact sport, and spectators into full participants.

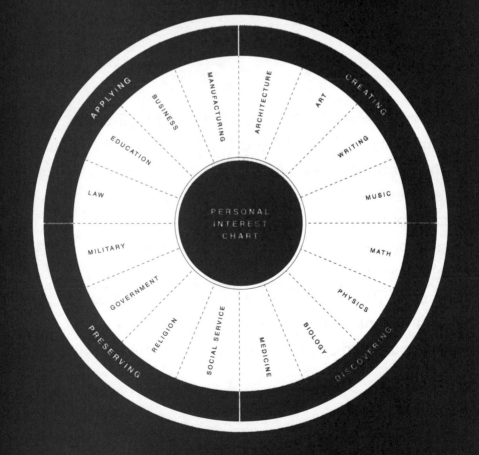

PEOPLE ARE DIFFERENT.

Over the last 15 years my firm has store-tested hundreds of package designs. When we first adopted this practice, the reactions of shoppers to our prototypes often differed in the extreme. One shopper would love design A, but hate—I mean HATE—design B. We began to realize that the audience for one product was likely to be different than the audience for another, and that its taste in design was also likely to be different. A little more delving revealed a fundamental split between two main personality types, those who relied mostly on hard information (facts) to make a purchase, and those who relied mostly on soft information (feelings).

Eventually we were able to diagram the shades of difference we found in the shoppers we encountered. The chart at the left divides the world into four mindsets, based on people's job interests: applying, creating, preserving, and discovering. "Appliers," for example, gravitate toward graphics that are precise, realistic, and familiar, while "creators" go for the lyrical, abstract, and novel. Guess what? If you divide the chart down the middle, you have an approximate map of the left and right brain.

TEST IS NOT A FOUR-LETTER WORD.

Unfortunately, audience research has gotten a bad rap from the creative community. It seems as if every third book on design and advertising contains a diatribe on the evils of market research. Such views are comforting to the creative crowd because they can absolve one's responsibility to everything but one's own artistic soul. As a creative person, I can bear witness to the seductive qualities of these anti-research arguments. And what makes them doubly seductive is that they're usually delivered by the superstars of their professions.

Any designer or advertising creative who has pored over stacks of research documents, or puzzled over the charts, graphs, and numerical detritis of serious marketing studies, may well conclude that researchers are paid by the page. The normal reaction of any red-blooded right-brainer is to politely take the documents, toss them in a corner, and get on with the job of being creative.

An aversion to research has been known in the boardrooms of some of the world's most innovative companies. Sony founder Akio Morita believed that testing new ideas was folly. "Our plan is to LEAD the public," he said. "They do not know what is possible." Even back in the command-and-control days of the production line, Henry Ford's decision to manufacture automobiles was driven by intuition rather than market research. "If we had asked the public what they wanted," he explained, "they would have said 'faster horses.'"

Innovators often feel that using research is like trying to chart the future in a rearview mirror. They've seen too many products and messages aimed where the audience was last sighted, instead of where it's likely to be tomorrow. Okay, creativity is subjective, but it's only subjective until it reaches the marketplace—then it's measurable. Ford's and Sony's innovations certainly were measured, not by research, but by the market itself.

But what if you could test your most innovative ideas BEFORE they got to market? Couldn't testing help you protect a potential breakthrough from the "fear of stupid"? Absolutely. And if you can't exactly PROVE that a concept will work, you can at least turn a wild guess into an educated one, and give your collaborators enough confidence to proceed. The direction of business is forward. Good research is the least amount of information that gets you out of first gear and onto the highway.

AN AVERSION TO AUDIENCE RESEARCH PAVED THE WAY FOR THE MONEY-LOSING EDSEL.

THE MYTH OF FOCUS GROUPS.

Whenever you mention audience research, people immediately think "focus group." Yet focus groups rarely deliver any of the consensus-building clarity needed to innovate. They were originally invented to FOCUS the research, not to BE the research. When used as a decision-making tool, they cast ordinary people in the role of professionals, and tend to elicit the received wisdom of a handful of alpha-consumers who see themselves as critics—and who would probably behave differently in a real buying situation. Focus groups are particularly susceptible to something called the Hawthorne effect—the tendency for people to act differently when they know they know someone's watching. In groups, it seems, some people just have to show off.

Focus groups are good as a starting point for quantitative research. Just don't use them to gauge sales, determine pricing, or analyze things like product design, package design, or messaging elements. What should you use instead? That depends on what you want to find out.

If you need to choose among prototypes, one-on-one interviews can give you enough insight to choose with confidence. If you're looking for an understanding of audience behavior, ethnographic observation can turn up some suggestive insights. A benefit of ethnography is that it tends to circumvent the Hawthorne effect by viewing human nature unobtrusively from the sidelines. As Yogi Berra said, "You'd be surprised by how much you can observe by watching."

THE SECRET OF AUDIENCE INSIGHT IS UNOBTRUSIVE OBSERVATION.

HOW TO AVOID GETTING SKEWED.

Often the first thing companies do when faced with a big decision is to order up a massive study. The bigger the better, because a large sample will minimize the "skew," or the degree of unreliability inherent in the study. What gets skewed instead is the thinking of the marketing team, because while quantitative research is long on numbers, it's short on insights, the little epiphanies that lead to break-throughs. Of course, if you just want to cover your butt, go for a big stack of quantitative data.

WITH RESEARCH,
MORE IS
OFTEN LESS.

Quantitative studies, while impressive, can lead to analysis paralysis when companies try to turn them into meaningful initiatives. Somehow all those numbers cause people to focus on small, measurable improvements that don't require any real courage, and in the end don't make much difference. Afterwards they provide a built-in excuse: "We tried that. It didn't work." It didn't work because it wasn't powered by heart-pounding insights. It went after small problems instead of hunting big game.

It's usually better to get a rough answer to the right question than a detailed answer to the wrong question. The truth is, most large studies could be cashed in for a series of smaller, more effective ones, and still have change left over. The best studies are quick and dirty—best not only because they save time and money, but because they're more likely to focus on one problem at a time. Why boil the ocean to make a cup of tea?

THE SWAP TEST.

Wanna check out the effectiveness of your brand icon? Here's a simple test you can perform without leaving your office. Swap part of your icon—the name or the visual element—with that of a competing brand, or even a brand from another category. If the resulting icon is better, or no worse than it was, your existing icon has room for improvement. By the same token, no other company should be able to improve its icon by using part of yours. A good brand icon is like a tailored suit—it should only look good on you.

DO THE TRADEMARKS FOR POLAROID AND NATIONWIDE FINANCIAL PASS THE SWAP TEST?

ORIGINAL TRADEMARKS

A variation on the swap test is the hand test. This quick-and-dirty proof lets you check the effectiveness of ads, brochures, web pages, and other brand communications. Take any piece of visual communication and cover up your trademark with your hand. Can you tell whose piece it is? If the communication in question looks as if it could have come from any other company or brand, then it's less than it could be. Because even without a trademark, those familiar with your brand should be able to tell who's talking just by its "voice," or the look and feel of the materials.

WITH NAMES SWAPPED

You have 206 bones in your body.
Surely, one of them is creative.

It doesn't take a lot of effort to enjoy digital music and movies – just the new iMac and a little creativity.

With Apple's award-winning iTunes software you can be your own DJ. iTunes makes it simple to "rip" your CDs and put your entire music collection right on your iMac. Just drag and drop to make playlists of your favorite songs. Listen to them on your iMac, or push one button to burn your own custom CDs that you can play in your car or portable CD player.

Or, for the ultimate in portability, get yourself an iPod. Just plug it into your iMac, and iTunes automatically downloads all your songs and playlists into iPod at blazing FireWire speed (an entire CD in a few seconds). Then just choose a pocket and take your entire music collection with you wherever you go.

For making movies, Apple's award-winning iMovie software lets you be the director. Plug your digital camcorder into iMac's FireWire port and transfer your video in pristine digital quality. Use iMovie's intuitive drag-and-drop interface to cut out the boring parts, add Hollywood-style effects – like cross-dissolves and scrolling titles – and lay in a soundtrack from your favorite CD. Then share your movies with friends and family by making a custom DVD using our aptly named SuperDrive and remarkable iDVD software! You'll be amazed at how professional your movies and DVDs look and how easy it is to create them.

With the new iMac, an ounce of creativity goes a very long way.

iPod. The first MP3 player to pack a mind-blowing 1,000 songs' and a 10-hour battery into a stunning 6.5-ounce package you can take with you wherever you go.

With iMovie and iDVD you can turn your movies into instant classics and create custom DVDs that play on almost any standard DVD player.

EVEN WITH THE TRADEMARK HIDDEN,
APPLE'S ADS, BROCHURES,
AND PRODUCTS ARE IDENTIFIABLE.

THE CONCEPT TEST.

Copywriter Steve Bautista wrote: "When people talk to themselves, it's called insanity. When companies talk to themselves, it's called marketing." How can you make sure your company isn't talking to itself? By closing the feedback loop—preferably BEFORE you take your concept to market. A simple concept test can help you develop names, symbols, icons, taglines, and brand promises by addressing two issues: 1) getting the right idea, and 2) getting the idea right. In other words, it not only helps you sort through a range of alternate approaches, it helps you polish the one you pick.

To test a concept, create a range of prototypes of the brand element in question. You can start with as many as seven concepts, but the most thoughtful responses will come when you get it down to two or three. (Like with a presidential election, people are most comfortable choosing between two candidates, and if necessary they can handle a third.)

Next, present the prototypes to at least 10 members of the real audience (not company insiders), one person at a time (not as a group). Then ask a series of questions like the ones below. Notice that nowhere in the questions will you find "Which one do you like?" It's not about liking. It's about understanding.

A brand promise, for example, might be illuminated by questions like these: Which of these promises is most valuable to you? Which company would you expect to make a promise like this? If company X made this promise, would that make sense? What other type of promise would you expect from company X? Always follow up with "Why?" because the answer to "why" will contain the seed of the next question.

You might test a brand icon with a slightly different set of questions: Which of these icons catches your eye first? What made you notice it? Does it remind you of any other icons you've seen? What do you think this particular icon means? If it's really supposed to mean X, do you think one of these other choices expresses it better? And so on.

1) GETTING THE **RIGHT** IDEA.

A significant advantage of a concept test is that it costs very little and yields results in a matter of hours or days, not weeks. Often, a concept test can be conducted online, using PDFs to present the images and a telephone call to conduct the interview. This "instant" feedback lets you conduct anywhere from one to three rounds—design plus testing—in less time than it would take to conduct one large study. Are concept tests conclusive? No, because they're not meant to be conclusive. They're meant to be lightning rods for insight. But if you want a larger sample, you can easily expand a concept test into full-scale quantitative study, which will then have the advantage of being focused on the real issues.

2) GETTING THE IDEA **RIGHT**.

True story: I once commissioned a worldwide brand study on behalf of Apple Computer. After spending a quarter-million dollars on a 10-city worldwide quantitative study, we ended up with virtually the same results as we got from our initial one-day test. Lesson: If you can live with a little uncertainty, an inexpensive concept test will often give you ample information to turn logic into magic.

IN THIS FIELD TEST, SHOPPERS WERE ASKED
WHICH CLARIS PACKAGE FIRST CAUGHT THEIR EYE.
MOST PICKED THE SPEEDING PENCIL.

THE FIELD TEST.

Prototypes that can be tested in a realistic situation offer the best feedback, because the mental leap from concept to reality is easier. For example, if you can test a packaging prototype on the shelf, next to the competition, using real shoppers who happen to be shopping your category, your results will be more accurate than if you conduct the test in a facility, using "incentivized" subjects who will naturally begin to think more about testing than shopping. In other words, you'll avoid getting skewed. The field test minimizes the Hawthorne effect by adhering more closely to normal shopping patterns.

Field tests can also be used to preview the success or failure of a new product. If the first point of contact between customer and product will be the store, then the store is where the product must first succeed. If the product comes in a package, then the package is where the product must succeed. Some of the most promising ideas have died quick and painful deaths, not because people didn't WANT them, but because the products didn't make sense at the point of contact. Happily, a field test can reveal fatal flaws BEFORE the product is launched, giving the team a chance to build a different package—or a different product.

Now it gets more interesting. What if a new product idea could be CONCEIVED at the packaging level? Instead of beginning in R&D, a product could begin with branding, first by building a set of prototypes for an imaginary product or package, and then by conducting an "opportunity test" at the point of contact. If the product looks like a winner where it counts most, in the customer's gut, then it can go to R&D for development. Remember, a brand is what THEY say it is, not what YOU say it is. Sometimes it makes sense to find out first, before you spend your whole development budget.

WHAT ARE WE LOOKING FOR?

Testing, or validation, is the process of measuring brands against meaningful criteria. All brand expressions, from icons to actual products, need to score high in five areas of communication: distinctiveness, relevance, memorability, extendibility, and depth.

DISTINCTIVENESS is the quality that causes a brand expression to stand out from competing messages. If it doesn't stand out, the game is over. Distinctiveness often requires boldness, innovation, surprise, and clarity, not to mention courage on the part of the company. Is it clear enough and unique enough to pass the swap test?

RELEVANCE asks whether a brand expression is appropriate for its goals. Does it pass the hand test? Does it grow naturally from the DNA of the brand? These are good questions, because it's possible to be attention-getting without being relevant, like a girly calendar issued by an auto parts company.

MEMORABILITY is the quality that allows people to recall the brand or brand expression when they need to. Testing for memorability is difficult, because memory proves itself over time. But testing can often reveal the presence of its drivers, such as emotion, surprise, distinctiveness, and relevance.

EXTENDIBILITY measures how well a given brand expression will work across media, across cultural boundaries, and across message types. In other words, does it have legs? Can it be extended into a series if necessary? It's surprisingly easy to create a one-off, single-use piece of communication that paints you into a corner.

DEPTH is the ability to communicate with audiences on a number of levels. People, even those in the same brand tribe, connect to ideas in different ways. Some are drawn to information, others to style, and still others to emotion. There are many levels of depth, and skilled communicators are able to create connections at most of them.

These are the criteria that validate brand design—they provide a reality check for breakthroughs. They not only separate true innovation from mere trendiness, they dispel the doubts that can freeze companies into inaction. When managers embrace the twin disciplines of innovation and validation, the marketing department is no longer the place where breakthrough ideas go to die. It's where they prosper and grow and multiply like magic.

TESTING MIGHT
HAVE SAVED
SOME OF THESE
COMPANIES FROM
THE 1999 SWOOSH
EPIDEMIC.

aroundcampus.com
your online survival guide!

PIX

bea

brightw

eCustomer Assistance

email messa

c

G.A.E
com

rivio

et Billing that Pays

eCstep

OpenSit

H

.CBN.COM

office

A SERVICE

viar

ySurf.com

PROVANT
The People Performance Company

INet

le the light

west.

edia

Trac

Telig

The Smart Wa

VIA

HAS THE GLOBE BECOME THE NEW SWOOSH?

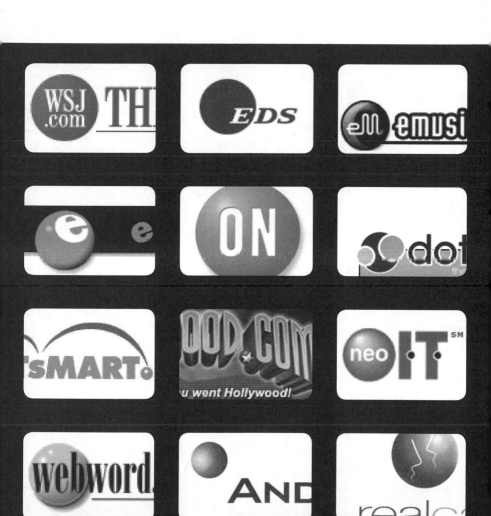

DISCIPLINE 5 : CULTIVATE

THE LIVING BRAND.

Business is a process, not an entity. Successful businesses are those that continually adapt to changes in the marketplace, the industry, the economy, and the culture. They behave more like organisms than organizations, shifting and growing and dividing and combining as needed. Unlike the old corporate identity paradigm that prized uniformity and consistency, the new brand paradigm sacrifices those qualities in favor of being alive and dynamic.

Perfection? It never existed. Control? Fuhgetaboudit. As entrepreneurial consultant Guy Kawasaki advises his clients: "Don't worry, be crappy." Let the brand live, breathe, make mistakes, be human. Instead of trying to present a Teflon-smooth surface, project a three-dimensional personality, inconsistencies and all. Brands can afford to be inconsistent—as long as they don't abandon their defining attributes. They're like people. For example, in the

IF **PEOPLE** CAN CHANGE THEIR CLOTHES TO SUIT THE OCCASION, WHY CAN'T **BRANDS**?

C.

D.

morning you can wear a T-shirt, and in the evening a dress shirt. One moment you can be serious, and the next laugh out loud. Despite these apparent inconsistencies in your dress and demeanor, your friends and colleagues will still recognize you. What makes you "you" is deeper than appearances and moods. I'll venture one step further, and say that

E.

F.

brands that don't project depth and humanity tend to create suspicion among customers.

The old paradigm in which identity systems try to control the "look" of an organization only result in cardboard characters, not three-dimensional protagonists. The new paradigm calls for heroes with flaws—living brands.

EVERY DAY YOU WRITE THE BOOK.

A living brand is a collaborative performance, and every person in the company is an actor. When a rep lands a customer, when an admin takes a phone call, when a CFO issues a profit warning, when a product manager gives a demo, when an accountant pays an invoice—each of these events adds depth and detail to the script, just as surely as a new ad campaign or website does. People "read" the script in their experiences with the company and its communications, then retell their version of it to others. When people's experiences match their expectations, their loyalty increases.

Drama coach Stella Adler often told her students, "Don't act. Behave." Living brands are not a stylistic veneer but a pattern of behavior that grows out of character. When the external actions of a company align with its internal culture, the brand resonates with authenticity. If a brand looks like a duck, quacks like a duck, walks like a duck, and swims like a duck, then it must be a duck. If it swims like a dog, however, people start to wonder.

DOES THE COMPANY'S BEHAVIOR
MATCH THE COMPANY'S IMAGE?

THE BRAND AS A COMPASS.

Let's say you've differentiated, collaborated, innovated, and validated. You've decided who you are, what you do, and why it matters. You've added the left brain to the right brain, and one plus one now equals eleven. You've zigged when the competition zagged, and you've ditched your outmoded logo for an distinctive brand icon. Finally, you've used audience feedback to banish the "fear of stupid" from your corporate culture. Your brand is heading up the charts with a loyal tribe of customers and collaborators, and your margins are higher than ever. What's your next move?

Pass out the compasses. Every person in the

EVERYONE IN THE COMPANY SHOULD HAVE A PERSONAL BRANDOMETER.

company should be issued a personal shockproof brandometer—a durable set of ideas about what the brand is and what makes it tick. Because no decision, big or small, should be made without asking the million-dollar question: "Will it help or hurt the brand?"

The secret of a living brand is that it lives throughout the company, not just in the marketing department. Since branding is a process, not an entity, it can be learned, taught, replicated, and cultivated. Continuing education programs can get everyone in the company onto the same page, while seminars, workshops, and critiques can keep outside collaborators singing in tune.

PROTECTING THE BRAND.

The growing importance of the brand has a flip side: its growing vulnerability. A failed launch, a wandering brand focus, or a whiff of scandal can damage credibility and decrease brand value. And now, thanks to globalization, bad news not only travels fast, it travels far. The Firestone tire fiasco quickly deflated the value of the Ford brand by 17%, from $36 billion down to $30 billion. And in one year alone Amazon lost 31% of its brand value in trying to extend its online book niche into an online bookmusiccameracomputerappliancebabyfurniture-toy niche—with predictable non-success. During the same period, the value of the Starbucks brand grew 32%. Why? Starbucks protected its brand as it reached its aromatic fingers further into middle-America, spreading the experience but keeping the focus tight.

For brand knowledge to become imbedded throughout the organization, it has to be protected against "evaporation," the tendency for decisional wisdom to disappear as experienced people leave the company. The long-term success of any brand depends on the constant regeneration of corporate memory. Since key people tend to stay in their positions only two to five years, the challenge is to capture brand knowledge and pass it to the next generation intact. How? With a brand education program that's distributed throughout the company and its creative network, guaranteeing the survival of the brand, while keeping it open to feedback from the brand community.

THIS SELECTION FROM INTERBRAND'S TOP 100 LIST SHOWS WHY BRANDS ARE WORTH PROTECTING:

BRAND NAME	BRAND VALUE IN MILLIONS OF DOLLARS	% CHANGE VS. PREVIOUS YEAR	BRAND VALUE AS % OF MARKET CAP
COCA-COLA	68,945	-5%	61%
MICROSOFT	65,068	-7%	17%
IBM	52,752	-1%	27%
FORD	30,092	-17%	66%
MERCEDES	21,728	+3%	48%
HONDA	14,638	-4%	33%
BMW	13,858	+7%	62%
KODAK	10,801	0%	65%
GAP	8,746	-6%	35%
NIKE	7,589	-5%	66%
PEPSI	6,214	-6%	9%
XEROX	6,019	-38%	93%
APPLE	5,464	-17%	66%
STARBUCKS	1,757	+32%	21%

WHERE ARE ALL THE CBOs?

As I said earlier, three basic models have evolved for managing large-scale creative collaboration. The first two are the paths of least resistance: outsourcing stewardship of the brand to a one-stop shop or a brand agency. The preference among advanced branders, however, is the third: internal stewardship of the brand with the help of an integrated marketing team. Intel's worldwide creative director, Susan Rockrise, calls this a "virtual agency," a concept she has pioneered for the better part of a decade. Intel, and other companies who favor the integrated marketing model, have learned how to recruit best-of-breed creative firms from around the world and get them to play together on an all-star team.

The more a brand becomes distributed, the more it requires strong, centralized management.

Creativity can quickly turn to chaos in the absence of adult supervision (as any parent knows). And while controlled chaos is necessary for innovation and change, uncontrolled chaos can make a brand schizophrenic and confused.

The growing need for internal stewardship has given rise to the appointment of what we might call chief brand officers, or CBOs—highly experienced professionals who manage brand collaboration at the highest corporate level. CBOs are rare birds, because they need the ability to strategize with the chief, and also inspire creativity among the troops. In effect they must form a human bridge across the brand gap, connecting the company's left brain with its right brain, bringing business strategy in line with customer experience. A CBO is the executive who lies awake at night thinking, "How can we build the brand?"

The main reason CBOs are rare is that few formal programs have been established to train them. Unlike CEOs, who can begin their careers with a degree in business administration, CBOs have to pick up their skills on the fly, working their knowledge

back and forth in various positions at advertising agencies, corporate marketing departments, design firms, and other creative and consulting businesses until they reach a level of mastery. While they may start their careers with a degree in marketing or design, neither program by itself can teach how to

combine logic and magic in the necessary propor-
tions. Those who do master this alchemy tend to
command middle-six-figure salaries in companies.
Fortunately, this has not gone unnoticed by progres-
sive business colleges and design schools, who
are now scrambling to catch up.

THE VIRTUOUS CIRCLE.

In the last century, many companies found themselves
trapped in a vicious circle of R&D investment, initial
market success, competitive pressure, and price-
cutting, until commoditization eventually forced them
out of the market.

Branding creates the opposite effect—a virtuous
circle. By combining logic and magic, a company
can ignite a chain reaction that leads from differentiation to collaboration to innovation to validation and
finally to cultivation. Built into cultivation is the man-
date to question all assumptions, leapfrog the status
quo, and begin the cycle again. With each turn, the
company and its brand spiral higher, taking it further
from commoditization and closer to the Holy Grail
of marketing: a sustainable competitive advantage.

A brand is not a logo. A brand is not a corporate
identity system. It's a person's gut feeling about a
product, service, or company. Because it depends
on others for its existence, it must become a guaran-
tee of trustworthy behavior. Good branding makes
business integral to society and creates opportunity
for everyone, from the chief executive to the most
distant customer.

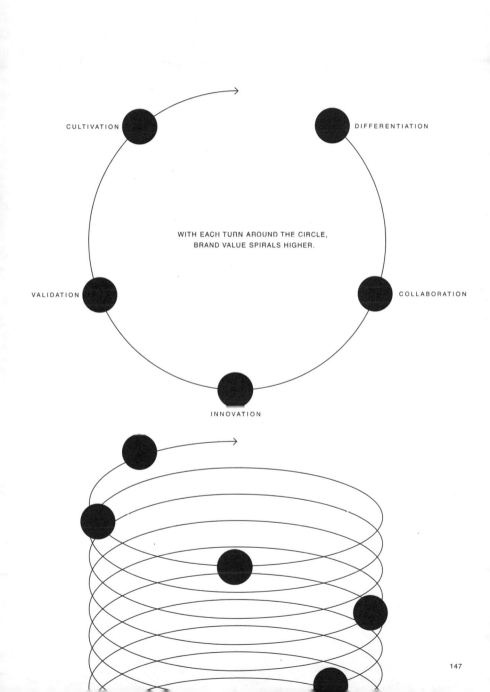

CULTIVATION

DIFFERENTIATION

WITH EACH TURN AROUND THE CIRCLE,
BRAND VALUE SPIRALS HIGHER.

VALIDATION

COLLABORATION

INNOVATION

TAKE-HOME LESSONS

Here's a quick summary of the ideas covered in THE BRAND GAP. Sprinkle liberally throughout your brand presentations, or try adding a different one to the bottom of each business e-mail you send—you may be surprised at the conversations you'll start.

→ A brand is a person's gut feeling about a product, service, or company. It's not what YOU say it is. It's what THEY say it is.

→ Branding is the process of connecting good strategy with good creativity. It's not the process of connecting good strategy with poor creativity, poor strategy with good creativity, or poor strategy with poor creativity.

→ The foundation of brand is trust. Customers trust your brand when their experiences consistently meet or beat their expectations.

→ Modern society is information-rich and time-poor. The value of your brand grows in direct proportion to how quickly and easily customers can say yes to your offering.

→ People base their buying decisions more on symbolic cues than features, benefits, and price. Make sure your symbols are compelling.

→ Only one competitor can be the cheapest—the others have to use branding. The stronger the brand, the greater the profit margin.

→ A charismatic brand is any product, service, or company for which people believe there's no substitute. Any brand can be charismatic, even yours.

DIFFERENTIATE

→ To begin building your brand, ask yourself three questions: 1) Who are you? 2) What do you do? 3) Why does it matter?

→ Our brains filter out irrelevant information, letting in only what's different and useful. Tell me again, why does your product matter?

→ Differentiation has evolved from a focus on "what it is," to "what it does," to "how you'll feel," to "who you are." While features, benefits, and price are still important to people, experiences and personal identity are even more important.

→ As globalism removes barriers, people erect new ones. They create tribes—intimate worlds they can understand and participate in. Brand names are tribal gods, each ruling a different space within the tribe.

→ Become the number one or number two in your space. Can't be number one or number two? Redefine your space or move to a different tribe.

COLLABORATE

→ Over time, specialists beat generalists. The winner is the brand that best fits a given space. The law of the jungle? Survival of the FITTINGEST.

→ How a brand should fit its space is determined
  by the brand community. It takes a village to
  build a brand.

→ By asking left-brainers and right-brainers to
  work as a team, you bridge the gap between
  logic and magic. With collaboration, one plus
  one equals eleven.

→ For successful precedents to creative collaboration, look to Hollywood, Silicon Valley, and
  the cathedral builders of the Renaissance.

→ As creative firms become more collaborative,
  they're also becoming more specialized.
  The next economy will see a rise in branding
  networks—groups of "unbundled" companies
  cooperating across the value chain.

→ Three basic models have emerged for managing brand collaboration: 1) the one-stop shop,
  2) the brand agency, and 3) the integrated
  marketing team. Choose any one or create
  a combination.

→ Speak in prototypes. Prototypes cut through marketing red tape and let gut feeling talk to gut feeling.

INNOVATE

→ It's design, not strategy, that ignites passion in people. And the magic behind better design and better business is innovation.

→ Radical innovation has the power to render competition obsolete. The innovator's mantra: When everyone zigs, zag.

→ How do you know when an idea is innovative? When it scares the hell out of you.

→ Expect innovation from people outside the company, or from people inside the company who THINK outside.

→ Make sure the name of your brand is distinctive, brief, appropriate, easy to spell, easy to pronounce, likable, extendible, and protectable.

→ Logos are dead. Long live icons and avatars.

→ Packaging is the last and best chance to influence a prospect this side of the checkout counter. Arrange all your packaging messages in a "natural reading sequence."

→ Avoid the three most common barriers to web innovation: technophobia, turfismo, and featuritis.

→ Bottom line: If it's not innovative, it's not magic.

VALIDATE

→ The standard communication model is an antique. Transform your brand communication from a monologue to a dialogue by getting feedback.

→ Feedback, i.e. audience research, can inspire and validate innovation.

→ Research has gotten an unfair rap from the creative community. Though bad research can be like looking at the road in a rearview mirror, good research can get brands out of reverse and onto the Autobahn.

→ Use focus groups to FOCUS the research, not BE the research. Focus groups are particularly susceptible to the Hawthorne effect, which happens when people know they're being tested.

→ Quantitative research is antithetical to inspiration. For epiphanies that lead to breakthroughs, use qualitative research.

→ Measure your company's brand expressions for distinctiveness, relevance, memorability, extendibility, and depth.

CULTIVATE

› Your business is not an entity but a living organism. Ditto your brand. Alignment, not consistency, is the basis of a living brand.

→ A living brand is a never-ending play, and every person in the company is an actor. People see the play whenever they experience the brand, and then they tell others.

→ Every brand contributor should develop a personal shockproof brandometer. No decision should be made without asking, "Will it help or hurt the brand?"

→ The growing importance of the brand has a flip side: its growing vulnerability. A failed launch, a drop in quality, or a whiff of scandal can damage credibility.

→ The more collaborative a brand becomes, the more centralized its management needs to be. The future of branding will require strong CBOs— chief brand officers who can steward the brand from inside the company.

→ Branding is a process that can be studied, analyzed, learned, taught, replicated, and managed.

It's the CBO's job to document and disseminate brand knowledge, and to transfer it whole to each new manager and collaborator.

→ Each lap around the branding circle, from differentiation to cultivation, takes the brand further from commoditization and closer to a sustainable competitive advantage.

Become a BRAND GAP GURU in your company. Visit **www.newriders.com** and download a free Adobe PDF presentation of the ideas in THE BRAND GAP. You can also buy discounted copies of THE BRAND GAP—an easy way to keep every member of your team focused on the company's brand.

BRAND GLOSSARY

Included in this revised edition is the complete list of definitions from THE DICTIONARY OF BRAND, a book I edited with the support of an all-star advisory council. The challenge was to create a "linguistic foundation"—a set of terms that allows specialists from different disciplines to work together in a larger community of practice. Neither the terms nor their definitions are carved in stone; we'll most certainly find that many are malleable, some are fluid, and a few are provisionary as we co-develop the practice of brand building.

ARTIFACT
A visible representation of an idea; a product or by-product of designing | see DESIGNING

ATMOSPHERICS
The identity of a brand environment, represented by its architecture, signage, textures, scents, sounds, colors, and employee behavior | see EXPERIENCE DESIGN

ATTITUDE STUDY
A survey of opinions about a brand, often used as a benchmark before and after making changes to it

AUDIENCE
The group to which a product, service, or message is aimed; also called the target audience

AUDIO BRANDING
The process of building a brand with auditory associations, such as Hewlett-Packard's use of the song "Pictures of You" in their Photosmart advertising | see EARCON

AUTHENTICITY
The quality of being genuine, often considered a powerful brand attribute

AVATAR
A brand icon designed to move, morph, or otherwise operate freely across various media | see ICON

AWARENESS STUDY
A survey that measures an audience's familiarity with a brand, often divided into "prompted" and "spontaneous" awareness | see AUDIENCE

BACKSTORY	The story behind a brand, such as its origin, the meaning of its name, or the underpinnings of its authenticity or charisma	see AUTHENTICITY, PROVENANCE
BENEFIT	A perceived advantage derived from a product, service, feature, or attribute
BHAG	A "Big, Hairy, Audacious Goal" designed to focus an organization	read BUILT TO LAST, Jim Collins and Jerry Porras
BOTTOM-UP MARKETING	Customer-driven marketing, as opposed to top-down or management-driven marketing	read BOTTOM-UP MARKETING, Al Ries and Jack Trout
BRAND	A person's perception of a product, service, experience, or organization; the art and science of brand building
BRAND AGENCY	A strategic firm that provides or manages a variety of brand-building services across a range of media
BRAND ALIGNMENT	The practice of linking brand strategy to customer touchpoints	see BRAND STRATEGY, TOUCHPOINT
BRAND AMBASSADOR	Anyone who promotes the brand through interactions with customers, prospects, partners, or the media; ideally, every company employee
BRAND ARCHITECTURE	A hierarchy of related brands, often beginning with a master brand, describing its relationship to subbrands and co-brands; a brand family tree	see CO-BRANDING, MASTER BRAND, SUBBRAND
BRAND ARTICULATION	A concise description of a brand that enables members of the brand community to collaborate; the brand story	see BRAND COMMUNITY, BRAND STORY
BRAND ASSET	Any aspect of a brand that has strategic value, which may include brand associations, brand attributes, brand awareness, or brand loyalty	see BRAND ATTRIBUTE, BRAND LOYALTY

BRAND ATTRIBUTE	A distinctive feature of a product, service, company, or brand
BRAND AUDIT	A formal assessment of a brand's strengths and weaknesses across all of its touchpoints │ see TOUCHPOINT
BRAND CHAMPION	Anyone who evangelizes or protects a brand; a brand steward │ see BRAND STEWARD
BRAND COMMUNITY	The network of people who contribute to building a brand, including internal departments, external firms, industry partners, customers, users, and the media
BRAND CONSULTANT	An external adviser who contributes to the brand-building process, often in a strategic or advisory role
BRAND COUNCIL	A committee formed to assess and guide a company's brand-building process; sometimes called a creative council
BRAND DESIGNER	Any person who helps shape a brand, including graphic designers, strategists, marketing directors, researchers, advertising planners, web developers, public relations specialists, copywriters, and others
BRAND EARNINGS	The share of a business's cash flow that can be attributed to the brand alone
BRANDED HOUSE	A company in which the dominant brand name is the company name, such as Mercedes Benz; also called a homogeneous brand or a monolithic brand; the opposite of a house of brands
BRAND EQUITY	The accumulated value of a company's brand assets, both financially and strategically; the overall market strength of a brand │ read MANAGING BRAND EQUITY, David A. Aaker
BRAND ESSENCE	The distillation of a brand's promise into the simplest possible terms

BRAND EXPERIENCE	All the interactions people have with a product, service, or organization; the raw material of a brand	see BRAND STORY
BRAND GAP	The gulf between business strategy and customer experience
BRAND IDENTITY	The outward expression of a brand, including its name, trademark, communications, and visual appearance	read DESIGNING BRAND IDENTITY, Alina Wheeler
BRAND IMAGE	A customer's mental picture of a product, service, or organization
BRANDING	Any effort or program to build a brand; the process of brand-building
BRAND LOYALTY	The strength of preference for a brand compared to competing brands, sometimes measured in repeat purchases
BRAND MANAGER	An obsolescent term for a person responsible for tactical issues facing a brand or brand family, such as pricing, promotion, distribution, and advertising; a product manager
BRAND MANUAL	A document that articulates the parameters of the brand for members of the brand community; a standardized set of brand-building tools	see BRAND COMMUNITY
BRANDMARK	An icon, avatar, wordmark, or other symbol for a brand; a trademark	see AVATAR, ICON, SYMBOL, TRADEMARK
BRAND METRICS	Measurements for monitoring changes in brand equity	see BRAND VALUATION
BRAND NAME	The verbal or written component of a brand icon; the name of a product, service, experience, or organization	see ICON

BRAND PERSONALITY	The character of a brand defined in human terms, such as Virgin = irreverent, or Chanel = refined
BRAND POLICE	Manager or team responsible for strict compliance with the guidelines in the brand manual | see BRAND MANUAL
BRAND PORTFOLIO	A suite of related brands; a collection of brands owned by one company | read BRAND PORTFOLIO STRATEGY, David A. Aaker
BRAND PUSHBACK	Marketplace resistance to brand messages or brand extensions, often leading to changes in brand strategy | see BRAND STRATEGY, EXTENSION
BRAND STEWARD	The person responsible for developing and protecting a brand
BRAND STORY	The articulation of a brand as a narrative; a coherent set of messages that articulate the meaning of a brand | see BACKSTORY
BRAND STRATEGY	A plan for the systematic development of a brand in order to meet business objectives
BRAND VALUATION	The process of measuring the monetary equity of a brand | see BRAND METRICS
BUZZ	The current public opinion about a product, service, experience, or organization | read THE ANATOMY OF BUZZ, Emanuel Rosen
CATEGORY	The arena in which a brand competes; a consideration set | see CONSIDERATION SET
CBO	A company's Chief Brand Officer, responsible for integrating the work of the brand community | see BRAND COMMUNITY
CHALLENGER BRAND	A new or rising brand that is viable in spite of competition from the dominant brand in its category | read EATING THE BIG FISH, Adam Morgan

CHARISMATIC BRAND	A brand that inspires a high degree of loyalty; also known as a lifestyle brand or passion brand ⎮ see TRIBAL BRAND
CLUTTER	The conceptual noise of the marketplace; a disorderly array of messages or elements that impedes understanding
CO-BRANDING	The purposeful linking of two or more brands for mutual benefit
CO-CREATION	The collaborative development of a product, service, brand, or message
COLLABORATION	The process by which people of different disciplines work in concert to build a brand; the practice of co-creation ⎮ read SERIOUS PLAY and NO MORE TEAMS!, Michael Schrage
COMMAND AND CONTROL	A management style relying on clearly defined goals, processes, and measurements; top-down rather than bottom-up or distributed management
COMMODITIZATION	The process by which customers come to see products, services, or companies as interchange-able, resulting in the erosion of profit margins; the opposite of brand-building ⎮ see VICIOUS CIRCLE
CONCEPT MAP	A diagram showing the connections among a set of concepts
CONCEPTUAL NOISE	Cognitive clutter arising from too many mes-sages or meanings; any competing ideas that undermine clarity ⎮ see CLUTTER
CONSIDERATION SET	The range of brands that a customer considers when making a purchase decision; a category ⎮ see CATEGORY
COOPETITION	The cooperation of two competitors so that both can win ⎮ read CO-OPETITION, Adam M. Brandenburger and Barry J. Nalebuff

CORE COMPETENCIES   A set of capabilities (typically two or three) that gives a company a strategic advantage

CORE IDENTITY   The central, sustainable elements of a brand identity, usually the name and trademark
| see **BRAND IDENTITY, TRADEMARK**

CORE IDEOLOGY   A combination of core values and core purpose
| see **CORE PURPOSE, CORE VALUES**

CORE PURPOSE   The reason a company exists beyond making a profit; part of a core ideology
| see **CORE IDEOLOGY**

CORE VALUES   An enduring set of principles that defines the ethics of a company; part of a core ideology
| see **CORE IDEOLOGY**

CORPORATE IDENTITY   The brand identity of a company, consisting of its visual identifiers such as the name, trademark, typography, and colors; a company's trade dress
| see **BRAND IDENTITY, TRADE DRESS**

CREATIVE BRIEF   A document that sets parameters for a brand-building project, including context, goals, processes, and budgetary constraints

CULTIVATION   The process of imbedding brand values throughout the organization; internal branding
| read **BUILDING THE BRAND-DRIVEN BUSINESS**, Aaker, Davis and Dunn

CULTURAL LOCK-IN   The inability of an organization to change its mental models in the face of clear market threats
| read **CREATIVE DESTRUCTION**, Richard N. Foster and Sarah Kaplan

CULTURE JAMMING   The act of modifying advertisements or brand messages to subvert their original intent; also known as subvertising | read **ADBUSTERS** magazine

CUSTOMER EXPECTATIONS   The anticipated benefits of a brand, whether explicit or implicit

CUSTOMER GOALS	The "jobs" that customers "hire" a product, service, experience, or organization to do for them ǀ read THE INNOVATOR'S SOLUTION, Christensen and Raynor
DESCRIPTOR	A term used with a brand name to describe the category in which the brand competes, such as "fluoride toothpaste" or "online bank" ǀ see CATEGORY
DESIGN	In brand-building, the planning or shaping of products, services, environments, systems, communications, or other artifacts to create a positive brand experience ǀ see ARTIFACT
DESIGNING	The process of design; bringing together strategic and creative processes to achieve a shared goal ǀ read WHY DESIGN?, published by AIGA
DESIGN MANAGEMENT	The practice of integrating the work of internal and external design teams to align brand expressions with strategic goals
DESIGN RESEARCH	Customer research on the experience and design of products or communication elements, using qualitative, quantitative, or ethnographic techniques ǀ see ETHNOGRAPHY, FIELD TEST, ONE-ON-ONE INTERVIEW
DIFFERENTIATION	The process of establishing a unique market position to increase profit margins and avoid commoditization; the result of positioning ǀ see POSITIONING ǀ read DIFFERENTIATE OR DIE, Jack Trout
DISRUPTIVE INNOVATION	A new product, service, or business that redefines the market; also called discontinuous innovation ǀ see FIRST MOVER ǀ read THE INNOVATOR'S DILEMMA, Clayton Christensen
DRIVE FEATURES	Brand attributes that are both important to customers and highly differentiated from those of competitors ǀ see BRAND ATTRIBUTE ǀ read THE MCKINSEY QUARTERLY, MAY 2004

DRIVER BRAND In a brand portfolio, the brand that drives a purchase decision, whether master brand, subbrand, or endorser brand
| see BRAND PORTFOLIO, ENDORSER BRAND, MASTER BRAND, SUBBRAND

EARCON An auditory brand symbol, such as United Airlines' use of "Rhapsody in Blue" as a brand expression; an aural icon | see ICON

ELEVATOR PITCH A one-sentence version of a brand's purpose or market position, short enough to convey during a brief elevator ride | see MARKET POSITION

EMERGENT ATTRIBUTE A feature, benefit, quality, or experience that arises from the brand, as opposed to the core product or service; an example is the friendliness of Google

EMOTIONAL BRANDING Brand-building efforts that aim at customers' feelings through sensory experiences
| read EMOTIONAL BRANDING, Marc Gobé and Sergio Zyman

ENDORSER BRAND A brand that promises satisfaction on behalf of a subbrand or co-brand, usually in a secondary position to the brand being endorsed
| see CO-BRANDING, SUBBRAND

ENVISIONED FUTURE A 10- to 30-year BHAG with vivid descriptions of what it will be like to reach the goal
| see BHAG | read BUILT TO LAST, Jim Collins and Jerry Porras

ETHNOGRAPHY The study of people in their natural settings; research to discover needs and desires that can be met with brand innovations

EXPERIENCE DESIGN A focus on shaping the experience of a customer or user, rather than on the artifacts themselves; the design of interactive media
| see ARTIFACT, INFORMATION ARCHITECT

EXTENDED IDENTITY	The elements that extend the core identity of a company or brand, organized into groupings such as brand personality, symbols, and positioning
	see BRAND PERSONALITY, CORE IDENTITY, POSITIONING, SYMBOL

EXTENSION	A new product or service that leverages the brand equity of a related product or service

EVANGELIST	A brand advocate, whether paid or unpaid

FEATURE	Any element of a product, service, or experience designed to deliver a benefit

FEATURE CREEP	The addition of unnecessary elements to a product, service, or experience; sometimes called featuritis

FIELD TEST	A type of qualitative research in which prototypes of products, packages, or messages are tested in real environments instead of laboratories
	see QUALITATIVE RESEARCH

FIFTH DISCIPLINE	The organizational discipline of systems thinking, used to integrate four other disciplines: personal mastery, mental models, shared vision, and team learning | read THE FIFTH DISCIPLINE, Peter Senge

FIRST MOVER	A company or brand that starts a new category
	see DISRUPTIVE INNOVATION

FOCUS GROUP	A qualitative research technique in which several people are invited to a research facility to discuss a given subject; a type of research designed to focus later research | see QUALITATIVE RESEARCH

FRANKENBRAND	A poorly aligned brand, often resulting from a merger or acquisition; a dysfunctional brand
	see BRAND ALIGNMENT

FUTURECASTING	A technique used to envision future products, industries, competitors, challenges, or opportunities; a combination of forecasting and imagination
	read UNSTUCK, Keith Yamashita and Sandra Spataro, Ph.D.

GENERIC	An unbranded product, service, or experience; a commodity | see COMMODITIZATION
GENERIC BRAND	A misnomer often applied to a commodity product or store brand (since the terms generic and brand are mutually exclusive) | see STORE BRAND
GLOBAL BRAND	A product, service, or company that competes globally (often a misnomer, since most brands, by definition, vary from culture to culture)
GUERILLA MARKETING	A marketing program that uses non-traditional channels to sell or advertise products or services | read GUERRILLA MARKETING, Jay Conrad Levinson
HALO BRAND	A brand that lends value to another brand by association, such as a well known master brand and lesser known subbrand
HARMONIZATION	The alignment of the elements of a brand across product lines or geographic regions
HAWTHORNE EFFECT	The tendency for research subjects to behave uncharacteristically | see OBSERVER EFFECT
HOLLYWOOD MODEL	A system of creative collaboration in which specialists work as a team for the duration of a project | see IMT, METATEAM, VIRTUAL AGENCY
HOUSE OF BRANDS	A company in which the dominant brand names are those of the products and services the company sells, also called a heterogeneous brand or pluralistic brand; the opposite of branded house
ICON	The visual symbol of a brand, usually based on a differentiated market position; a trademark | see TRADEMARK
IMT	An Integrated Marketing Team, comprised of various specialist firms collaborating to build a brand; a metateam or virtual agency | see HOLLYWOOD MODEL, METATEAM, VIRTUAL AGENCY

INFORMATION ARCHITECT	A person who designs complex information systems to make them more navigable | read INFORMATION ARCHITECTS, edited by Richard Saul Wurman
INFORMATION HIERARCHY	The order of importance of the elements in a brand message
INGREDIENT BRAND	A brand used as a selling feature in another brand
INNOVATION	A market-changing product, service, experience, or concept; the formal practice of innovation | read THE ART OF INNOVATION, Tom Kelley et al.
INTEGRATED MARKETING	A collaborative method for developing consistent messaging across media
INTELLECTUAL PROPERTY	Intangible assets protected by patents and copy-rights; the legal discipline that specializes in the protection of brand assets, including brand names, trademarks, colors, shapes, sounds, and smells
INTERNAL BRANDING	An internal program to spread brand understanding through the use of standards manuals, orientation sessions, workshops, critiques, and online training; brand cultivation
JAMMING	Building a brand or company through improvisa-tional collaboration | read JAMMING, John Kao
JUNK BRAND	A brand based on a facade instead of a real value proposition; sometimes called a Potemkin brand | see VALUE PROPOSITION
LEVERAGING A BRAND	Borrowing from the credibility of one brand to launch another brand, subbrand, or co-brand; a brand extension | see CO-BRANDING, SUBBRAND
LINE EXTENSION	The addition of one or more subbrands to a master brand; the expansion of a brand family | see MASTER BRAND, SUBBRAND

BRAND GLOSSARY

LIVING BRAND	A brand that grows, changes, and sustains itself; a healthy brand
LOGO	An abbreviation of logotype, now applied broadly (if incorrectly) to all trademarks | see LOGOTYPE, TRADEMARK
LOGOTYPE	A distinctive typeface or lettering style used to represent a brand name; a wordmark
LOOK AND FEEL	The sensory experience of a product, environment, or communication
MALL INTERCEPT	A market research technique in which researchers interview customers in a store or public location; a one-on-one interview | see ONE-ON-ONE INTERVIEW
MARKETING	The process of developing, promoting, selling, and distributing a product or service | read THE 22 IMMUTABLE LAWS OF MARKETING, Al Ries
MARKETING AESTHETICS	The principles of perception used to enhance the feelings or experiences of an audience | read MARKETING AESTHETICS, Bernd Schmitt and Alex Simonson
MARKET PENETRATION	The market share of a product, service, or company compared to others in the category
MARKET POSITION	The ranking of a product, service, or company within a category, sometimes calculated as market share multiplied by share of mind | see POSITIONING
MARKET SHARE	The percentage of total sales in a given category, usually expressed in the number of units sold or the value of units sold | see MARKET POSITION
MASTER BRAND	The dominant brand in a line or across a business, such as Pepperidge Farm or Sony, to which subbrands can be added; a parent brand | see BRAND ARCHITECTURE, PARENT BRAND, SUBBRAND

MEDIA	The channels through which brand messages are delivered, such as television, printed publications, direct mail, the Internet, and outdoor posters
MEDIA ADVERTISING	One-way messages designed to sell, persuade, or create awareness of a brand through public communication channels
MEME	An idea that self-reproduces like a virus; a unit of social currency, such as "Where's the beef?" or "Sweet!" | read THE SELFISH GENE, Richard Dawkins
MENTAL MODEL	A conceptual image of an experience, environment, process, or system that provides better understanding or predictive value
MESSAGE ARCHITECTURE	The formal relationships among brand communications
METATEAM	A large team made up of smaller specialist teams; an IMT or virtual agency | see HOLLYWOOD MODEL, IMT, VIRTUAL AGENCY
MISSION STATEMENT	A concise statement of the purpose or aspirations of an organization
MORPHEME	The smallest unit of language that has meaning, often used by naming specialists to assemble coined words, or neologisms | see NEOLOGISM
NAME BRAND	A widely recognized product, service, or organization
NATURAL READING SEQUENCE	The order in which readers can most easily absorb separate pieces of information
NEOLOGISM	A coined word or phrase that can serve as a brand name | see MORPHEME

| **NEW LUXURY** | Goods and services that deliver higher quality or superior performance at a premium price, such as Belvedere Vodka or Callaway Golf Clubs |
| | read TRADING UP, Michael J. Silverstein and Neil Fiske |

| **NIH SYNDROME** | The tendency of a company, department, employee, or consultant to reject any idea "Not Invented Here" |

| **NO-LOGO MOVEMENT** | A group of activists who see global brands as a form of cultural imperialism | read NO LOGO, Naomi Klein |

| **NOMENCLATURE SYSTEM** | A formal structure for naming related products, services, features, or benefits; the naming portion of an organization's brand architecture |
| | see BRAND ARCHITECTURE |

| **OBSERVER EFFECT** | A tendency for the presence of the observer to change what is being observed | see HAWTHORNE EFFECT |

| **ONE-ON-ONE INTERVIEW** | A market research technique in which subjects are interviewed one at a time |

| **ONE-STOP SHOP** | A single firm that offers a full range of branding services, as opposed to an IMT | see IMT |

| **OPINION LEADER** | A person whose opinion or personality exerts an influence over other members of a group; also called an opinion maker |

| **PARALLEL EXECUTION** | The process by which creative teams work simultaneously rather than sequentially |

| **PARENT BRAND** | The main brand in a brand family; a master brand |
| | see BRAND ARCHITECTURE, MASTER BRAND |

| **PERCEPTION** | An impression received through the senses; a building block of customer experience |
| | see MARKETING AESTHETICS |

| **PERCEPTUAL MAP** | A diagram of customer perceptions showing the relationships between competing products, service, companies, or brands |

PERMANENT MEDIA	Environmental brand messages that last for years, such as architecture or signage
PERMISSION MARKETING	The practice of promoting goods or services with anticipated, personal, and relevant messages ❘ read **PERMISSION MARKETING**, Seth Godin
POSITIONING	The process of differentiating a product, service, or company in a customer's mind to obtain a strategic competitive advantage; the first step in building a brand ❘ read **POSITIONING**, Al Ries and Jack Trout
POWER LAW	In brand building, the tendency for success to attract more success; a law that explains why the "rich get richer" ❘ see **VIRTUOUS CIRCLE**
PRIMACY EFFECT	The observation that first impressions tend to be stronger than later impressions, except for last impressions ❘ see **RECENCY EFFECT**
PRIVATE LABEL	A store-owned product that competes, often at a lower price, with widely distributed products; a store brand as opposed to a name brand ❘ see **NAME BRAND, STORE BRAND**
PRODUCT PLACEMENT	A form of paid advertising in which products and trademarks are inserted into non-advertising media such as movies, television programs, music, and public environments
PROMISE	A stated or implied pledge that creates customer expectations and employee responsibilities, such as FedEx's on-time guarantee
PROSUMER	A category of products and services that combines professional-level features with consumer-level usability and price
PROTOTYPE	A model, mockup, or plan used to evaluate or develop a new product, service, environment, communication, or experience

PROVENANCE	A historical connection that lends authenticity or credibility to a brand	see AUTHENTICITY
PURE PLAY	A company with a single line of business; a highly focused brand
QUALIA	Subjective experiences that determine how each person perceives a brand	see EXPERIENCE DESIGN
QUALITATIVE RESEARCH	Research designed to provide insight, such as one-on-one interviews and focus groups	see DESIGN RESEARCH, FOCUS GROUP, ONE-ON-ONE INTERVIEW
QUANTITATIVE RESEARCH	Research designed to provide measurement, such as polling and large-scale studies	see DESIGN RESEARCH
RADICAL DIFFERENTIATION	A bold position that allows a brand to stand out from market clutter; a zag	see POSITIONING, ZAG
RAPID PROTOTYPING	A process of producing quick rounds of mockups, models, or concepts in rapid succession, evaluating and reiterating after each round to develop more effective products, services, or experiences	read THE ART OF INNOVATION, Tom Kelley et al.
REACH	The number of people exposed to an advertising or brand message	see MARKET PENETRATION
RECENCY EFFECT	The observation that last impressions tend to be stronger than earlier impressions, including first impressions	see PRIMACY EFFECT
REPUTATION	The shared opinion of a product, service, or organization among all the members of its audience	see AUDIENCE
SACRIFICE	The practice of eliminating any product, service, or feature that fails to strengthen a market position or brand

SALES CYCLE   For buyers, the steps in making a purchase (often defined as awareness, consideration, decision, and use); for sellers, the steps in making a sale (often defined as finding and qualifying customers, defining the products or services, and accepting and acknowledging the order)

SEGMENT   A group of people who are likely to respond to a given marketing effort in a similar way | see AUDIENCE

SEGMENTATION   The process of dividing a market into subcategories of people who share similar values and goals

SHELF IMPACT   The ability of a product, package, or brand to stand out on a shelf by virtue of its design

SIGNATURE   The defined visual relationship between a logotype and a symbol | see LOGOTYPE, SYMBOL

SILO   A department separated from other departments according to product, service, function, or market; a disparaging term for a non-collaborative department

SLOGAN   A catchphrase, tagline, or rally cry; from the Gaelic "sluagh-ghairm," meaning "war cry"

SOCIAL NETWORK   A network of people that can be leveraged to spread ideas or messages using viral marketing techniques | see VIRAL MARKETING

SOCK-PUPPET MARKETING   A disparaging term for "fake" brands built on frothy advertising campaigns, such as those of the dot-com era
| read THE FALL OF ADVERTISING, Al Ries and Laura Ries

SPECIALIZATION   The strategy of focusing and deepening a business offering to better compete with larger companies or to better collaborate with other specialists

SPEECH-STREAM VISIBILITY The quality of a brand name that allows it to be recognized as a proper noun (as opposed to a generic word) in conversation, such as Kodak or Smuckers

STAKEHOLDER Any person or firm with a vested interest in a company or brand, including shareholders, employees, partners, suppliers, customers, and community members

STORE BRAND A private-label product that can be sold at lower prices or higher margins than its widely distributed competitors, sometimes incorrectly called a generic brand; a private-label brand
| see GENERIC BRANDS, PRIVATE LABEL

STRATEGIC DNA A decision-making code derived from the intertwining of business strategy and brand strategy

STRATEGY A plan that uses a set of tactics to achieve a business goal, often by out-maneuvering competitors
| see BRAND STRATEGY

SUBBRAND A secondary brand that builds on the associations of a master brand | see MASTER BRAND

SUSTAINING INNOVATION An incremental improvement to an existing product, service, or business | see DISRUPTIVE INNOVATION

SWOT A conceptual tool that analyzes Strengths, Weaknesses, Opportunities, and Threats

SYMBOL A sign or trademark designed to represent a brand

TACTIC An expedient maneuver used in support of a strategy

TAGLINE A sentence, phrase, or word used to summarize a market position, such as Mini's "Let's motor" and Taco Bell's "Think outside the bun"
| see POSITIONING, SLOGAN

TARGET MARKET The group of customers a company has decided to serve | see SEGMENTATION

TEAM DYNAMICS The psychological factors that influence collaboration, including trust, fear, respect, and company politics | read UNSTUCK, Keith Yamashita and Sandra Spataro, Ph.D.

THOUGHT LEADER A brand that leads the market in influential ideas, though not necessarily in market share, such as Apple Computer

TIPPING POINT A leverage point in the evolution of a market or society where a small effort can yield a surprisingly large result, not unlike "the straw that breaks the camel's back" | read THE TIPPING POINT, Malcolm Gladwell

TOUCHPOINT Any place where people come in contact with a brand, including product use, packaging, advertising, editorial, movies, store environments, company employees, and casual conversation

TRADE DRESS The colors, shapes, typefaces, page treatments, and other visual properties that create a recognizable "face" for a brand | see BRAND IDENTITY

TRADEMARK A name and/or symbol that indicates a source of goods or services and prevents confusion in the marketplace; a legally protectable form of intellectual property | read DESIGNING BRAND IDENTITY, Alina Wheeler

TRIBAL BRAND A brand with a cult-like following, such as Harley-Davidson, eBay, or American Idol

TURFISMO The tendency of managers to protect their autonomy at the expense of collaboration

TV-INDUSTRIAL COMPLEX The dominant system for launching and sustaining national brands during the last half of the 20th century, now weakened by the spread of new media and tribal brands
| see TRIBAL BRAND | read PURPLE COW, Seth Godin

USP The Unique Selling Proposition of a product or service, as championed by advertising executive Rosser Reeves in the 1950s; a type of differentiation | see DIFFERENTIATION

VALIDATION Customer approval or feedback for a proposed message, concept, or prototype | see PROTOTYPE

VALUE PROPOSITION A set of benefits, including functional, emotional, and self-expressive benefits

VICIOUS CIRCLE In brand strategy, a death spiral that leads from a lack of differentiation to lower prices, to smaller profit margins, to fewer available resources, to less innovation, to even less differentiation, and finally to commoditization; the opposite of a virtuous circle

VIRAL MARKETING A technique by which social networks are used to spread ideas or messages, through the use of affiliate programs, co-branding, e-mails, and link exchanges on-line, or off-line, through use of word-of-mouth advertising and memes
| see MEME | read UNLEASHING THE IDEAVIRUS, Seth Godin

VIRTUAL AGENCY A team of specialist firms that work together to build a brand, coined by Susan Rockrise of Intel; also called an IMT or metateam
| see HOLLYWOOD MODEL, IMT, METATEAM

VIRTUOUS CIRCLE The opposite of a vicious circle; a growth spiral that leads from differentiation, to higher prices, to larger profit margins, to more available resources, to more innovation, to further differentiation, and then to a sustainable competitive advantage

VISION The story a leader tells about where an organization is going; the aspirations of a company that drive future growth

ZAG A contrarian strategy that yields a competitive advantage; the differentiating idea that drives a charismatic brand | see CHARISMATIC BRAND

RECOMMENDED READING

The ideas in **THE BRAND GAP** are like a group of islands whose foundations extend below the surface of the page: What you see are only the peaks. Yet I hope I've roused your sense of adventure enough so you'll dive deeper into brand and its five disciplines. Here are a few titles I've found rewarding and true, together with brief descriptions.

GENERAL BRANDING

BRAND LEADERSHIP, David A. Aaker and Erich Joachimsthaler (Free Press, 2000). To be successful, say the authors, a brand must be led from the top. This shift from a tactical approach to a strategic approach requires an equal shift in organizational structure, systems, and culture. The authors prove their point with hundreds of examples from Virgin to Swatch and from Marriot to McDonald's.

BRAND PORTFOLIO STRATEGY, David A. Aaker (Free Press, 2004). David Aaker has spent more than a decade building a taxonomy of brand theory, helping to define and categorize all the dependencies needed for managing brands. Here he turns his attention from single brands to families of brands, showing how to stretch a brand without breaking it, and how to grow a business without unfocusing it.

BRAND WARFARE, David D'Alessandro (McGraw-Hill Trade, 2001). The author tells how he brought his branding skills to a job as CEO of John Hancock, transforming the sleepy life insurer into a leading financial services giant. He explains why the brand must always take priority over every other business consideration, becoming a prism through which every decision must be filtered.

EMOTIONAL BRANDING, Marc Gobé (Allworth Press, 2001). Creating emotion, aesthetics, and experience are the province of brand practitioners like Gobé, who uses his company's portfolio to illustrate and expand upon the work of Aaker and Schmitt, showing how logic and magic are expressed in the practice of design.

MANAGING BRAND EQUITY, David A. Aaker (Free Press, 1991). Aaker fired the first salvo in the brand revolution by proving that names, symbols, and slogans are valuable—and measurable—strategic assets. He followed this book with another called **BUILDING STRONG BRANDS** (Free Press, 1995), which escalated the conversation by introducing the role of emotion in creating brand power. Aaker's books provide the homework that underpins modern brand thinking.

MARKETING AESTHETICS, Bernd H. Schmitt and Alex Simonson (Free Press, 1997). Schmitt and Simonson take Aaker's thesis one step further by showing that aesthetics is what drives emotion. Schmitt forged onward with **EXPERIENTIAL MARKETING** (Free Press, 1999), in which he focused on the importance of customer experience in building a brand.

SELLING THE INVISIBLE, Harry Beckwith (Warner Books, 1997). A veteran of advertising, Beckwith takes on the toughest branding conundrum, how to market products that people can't see—otherwise known as services. His follow-up book, **THE INVISIBLE TOUCH** (Warner Books, 2000), lays out the four keys of modern marketing: price, branding, packaging, and relationships. Those who sell tangible products would do well to master many of the same principles: If you can sell the invisible, the visible is a piece of cake. Both books are delightful and memorable.

DIFFERENTIATION

BUILT TO LAST, James C. Collins and Jerry I. Porras (HarperBusiness Essentials, 1994). Brands may not last, but companies can, say Collins and Porras. The key to longevity is to preserve the core and stimulate progress. What's the core of your business? Your value set? Your promise? This is the place where true differentiation starts, whether your company is a house of brands or a branded house. The authors spent six years on research, which gives the book a certain gravitas.

POSITIONING: THE BATTLE FOR YOUR MIND, Al Ries and Jack Trout (McGraw-Hill Trade, 2000). POSITIONING started as a brochure in the early 1970s, then grew into a book, and has been continuously updated without ever losing its salience. Ries and Trout pioneered the concept of positioning, the Big Bang of differentiation which soon they expanded into a dozen or more books, each viewing the subject from a different angle. If you can grasp the simple truths in this body of work, you'll understand 90% of what marketing people don't—the customer decides the brand.

PURPLE COW, Seth Godin (Portfolio, 2003). The author likens a differentiated brand to a purple cow. When driving through the countryside, the first brown cow gets your attention. After ten or twelve brown cows, not so much. Godin proves his point with innumerable examples from today's brandscape, and shows how any company can stand out from the herd. He also takes aim at advertising as usual, proclaiming the death of the TV-industrial complex. It's time to mooove on, folks.

COLLABORATION   **NO MORE TEAMS!**, Michael Schrage (Currency/ Doubleday, 1995). Teamwork has only been given lip service until now, argues Schrage, and for teams to be innovative they need "shared spaces" and collaborative tools. Well written and highly original, NO MORE TEAMS! will bring you closer to your ultimate goal, breakthrough concepts that can revolutionize a business or even a whole industry, and create a sustainable competitive advantage.

ORGANIZING GENIUS, Warren Bennis and Patricia Ward Biederman (Perseus Publishing, 1998). An expert on leadership skills, Bennis shows how to unleash the creative potential of teamwork within the organization. A seminal work on the subject, and highly inspirational.

SIX THINKING HATS, Edward de Bono (Little, Brown and Company, 1985). When executives try to brainstorm the future of their organization, the discussion can quickly turn to disagreement. Edward de Bono, acknowledged master of thinking skills, shows how to get the group's best ideas by focusing on one kind of thinking at a time. By organizing the session into a series of "hats", i.e., red for emotions, black for devil's advocate, green for creativity, ideas aren't shot down before they're proposed. I've used this system with my clients with remarkable results.

UNSTUCK, Keith Yamashita and Sandra Spataro, Ph.D. (Portfolio, 2004). As we move from the century of the individual to the century of the team, the game of business is shifting to a new level of complexity. Frustrated team members (feeling alone, overwhelmed, directionless, battle-torn, worthless, hopeless, exhausted?) can use the exercises in this book to work free of their stuckness. If you like the chart-laden design of THE BRAND GAP, you'll love the design of UNSTUCK.

THE ART OF INNOVATION, Tom Kelley et al. (Currency/Doubleday, 2000). Kelley pulls back the curtain at IDEO to reveal the inner workings of today's premier product design firm. He shows how the firm uses brainstorming and prototyping to design such innovative products as the Palm V, children's "fat" toothbrushes, and wearable electronics. Cool stuff!

DESIGNING BRAND IDENTITY, Alina Wheeler (Wiley, 2003). This is the new bible for creating the look and feel of a brand. Step by step, touchpoint by touchpoint, Wheeler shows how to turn brand strategy into a perfect customer experience.

EATING THE BIG FISH, Adam Morgan (John Wiley & Sons, 1999). Only one brand can be number one, says Morgan, which means the others have to try harder. He details the traits common to "challenger" brands, which include the courage to be different and the smarts to be innovative. Plenty of real-world examples show that Morgan's principles are based in practice, not theory.

SERIOUS PLAY, Michael Schrage (Harvard Business School Press, 1999). Schrage isn't kidding—he seriously wants you to adopt a collaborative model. He says the secret is building quick-and-dirty prototypes, which serve as shared spaces for innovation. He brings the reader into the wild world of the right-brain, where play equals seriousness, and serious players work on fun-loving teams.

A SMILE IN THE MIND, Beryl McAlhone and David Stuart (Phaidon, 1996). If you were to buy only one book on graphic design, this would be it. Designer Stuart and writer McAlhone prove that wit is the soul of innovation, using clever and often profound examples from American and European designers, plus a modest few pieces from Stuart's own talented firm, The Partners, based in London.

BOTTOM-UP MARKETING, Al Ries and Jack Trout (Plume, 1989). The concept of building a brand from the bottom up is stunning in its simplicity. The authors advise starting at the customer level to find a tactic that works, then building the tactic into a strategy—instead of the other way around. Next thing you know they'll advocate turning the org chart upside down. Hmmm—wait a minute...

HITTING THE SWEET SPOT, Lisa Fortini-Campbell (Copy Workshop, 1992). To hit the sweet spot, you need the right ratio of brand insight to consumer insight. Combining theory with practical exercises, the author shows how to take market research from data, to information, to insight, and finally to inspiration.

STATE OF THE ART MARKETING RESEARCH, George Breen, Alan Dutka, and A. B. Blankenship (McGraw-Hill, 1998). This is probably more than you'll ever want to know about marketing research—unless you're a professional researcher—including how to do mall interviews, focus groups, and mail studies. But if you need a good reference on the subject (or if you think only on the left side), this is your book.

TRUTH, LIES AND ADVERTISING, Jon Steel (John Wiley & Sons, 1998). Steel was an account planner at Goodby, Silverstein & Partners, the agency famous for the "Got milk?" campaign and many others. Part researcher, part account executive, part agency creative, and part surrogate customer, he shows how to get inside customers' minds to discover how they relate to brands, products, and categories.

THE AGENDA, Michael Hammer (Crown Business, 2001). Sustained execution is the key to long-term success, says business guru Hammer, author of RE-ENGINEERING THE CORPORATION. He spells out a nine-point action plan, including "systematize creativity", "profit from the power of ambiguity", and "collaborate whenever you can". While focused more on leadership than on marketing, Hammer's plan aligns perfectly with the best practices of brand building.

BUILDING THE BRAND-DRIVEN BUSINESS, Scott M. Davis and Michael Dunn (Jossey-Bass, 2002). It's all about controlling the touchpoints, those places where customers experience the brand. Davis and Dunn tell how to segment those experiences into pre-purchase, during-purchase, and post-purchase, so that everyone in the organization knows their role in building the brand.

LIVING THE BRAND, Nicholas Ind (Kogan Page, 2001). A company's workforce is its most valuable asset, says Ind, who recommends a participatory approach to branding. He shows how meaning, purpose, and values can be built into the organization to turn every employee into a champion for the brand.

WILL AND VISION, Gerard Tellis and Peter Golder (McGraw-Hill Trade, 2001). To marketers who subscribe to the theory of the first mover advantage, Tellis and Golder say "Not so fast!" They use an impressive number of case studies, including Gillette, Microsoft, and Xerox, to isolate five key principles needed to build enduring brands: vision of the mass market, managerial persistence, relentless innovation, financial commitment, and asset leverage.

ACKNOWLEDGMENTS A theme of this book is that brands don't evolve in isolation—they require the talents of many people. Books don't evolve in isolation, either. **THE BRAND GAP** is the result of many hours of conversation with people who are impassioned by design and business. The book took two years to research, write, and design; I couldn't have done it in twenty years without their help.

My litany begins with Michael Nolan of New Riders, who started the ball rolling by believing I could write a book on brand design. He kept the notion alive for a year while I finished other projects, and when I finally got down to work, his support was constant. Thanks also to publisher David Dwyer and associate publisher Stephanie Wall for insisting that the book stay true to its original vision.

A warm nod to Nancy Bernard, my trusted associate and former co-editor of CRITIQUE magazine, who helped me hone my thoughts over the many months they took to formulate. In the end, either of us could have written the book.

David Stuart was instrumental in opening my eyes to the growing importance of creative collaboration. His London design firm, The Partners, has for years practiced what I preach, routinely combining logic and magic for the benefit of their clients and their clients' customers.

Greg Galle of the brand firm C2, with characteristic brilliance and rigor, lent his thoughts to the book, then combed the text for specious arguments, gratuitous observations, and other nits that annoy the careful reader.

Thanks to Susan Rockrise, who graciously agreed to become the poster girl for brand collaboration while giving me the benefit of her experience as worldwide creative director at Intel. She's one of the few people who can manage 50 creative firms as if they were one.

My gratitude and admiration to all those who contributed their talents to the making of the book, including Heather McDonald for the design of the interior, Chris Willis for the cover, Chris Chu for his early concepts, and Jeanne Carley for her excellent photography.

The text was improved enormously by the comments of critics, clients, and colleagues who took time to review the prototype. Appreciative bows to David Aaker, Jerry Bertrand, Karen Bollinger, Robin Brandenburg, Bill Cahan, Kerry Foster, Patrick Fricke, Gary Gleason, Richard Grefé, Tom Kelley, Clement Mok, Elizabeth Olsen, David Parks, Jim Peterson, Rob Rodin, Barrie Schwortz, Peter Van Naarden, and my good friend Gordon Mortensen.

Special thanks to my brand-glossary advisory council: Jeremy Bullmore of the advertising organization WPP, Hugh Dubberly of the interactive firm Dubberly Design Office, Tom Kelley of the product design firm IDEO, Davis Masten of Cheskin Research, marketing author Seth Godin, positioning author Al Ries, Susan Rockrise of Intel, collaboration author Michael Schrage, brand-identity author Alina Wheeler, and the "vision designers" from Stone Yamashita Partners. Outside the council, a number of colleagues from the AIGA Center for Brand Experience helped in herding the right words onto the page.

Of the 220 glossary terms, many have been introduced by authors, in which case I tried to include the titles of their books. You can find some of them listed in the preceding recommended reading section.

I've been extremely lucky in that most of my projects, including this one, have been labors of love. Thanks to my mother Lorna, for revealing the joy in everything and everyone; to my father Gene, for teaching me to try; to my brother Peter, for his steady counsel; to Francele, Marianne, Ellyn, and Carla, for being the best sisters anyone could have; to my daughter Sara, for her generous spirit; and, finally, to Eileen, my amazing wife of 36 years.

INDEX

ABOUT THE AUTHOR

Marty Neumeier is Director of Transformation at Liquid Agency, a firm that develops programs to spur strategic innovation, build charismatic brands, and transform organizational culture.

Neumeier began his career as a designer, but soon added writing and strategy to his repertoire, working variously as an identity designer, art director, copywriter, journalist, package designer, magazine publisher, and brand consultant. By the mid-1990s he had developed hundreds of brand icons, retail packages, and other communications for companies such as Apple Computer, Adobe Systems, Netscape Communications, Eastman Kodak, and Hewlett-Packard.

In 1996 he launched CRITIQUE, the magazine of design thinking, which quickly became the leading forum for improving design effectiveness through critical analysis. In editing CRITIQUE, Neumeier joined the growing conversation about bridging the gap between business strategy and customer experience, which led directly to the formation of the management consulting firm Neutron and the ideas in his series of "whiteboard overview" books.

Neutron merged with Liquid Agency in 2009, creating a new firm that offers "inside-out" brand transformation services that include culture-change roadmaps and comprehensive brand marketing programs resulting in significant improvements in a company's ability to compete and grow through nonstop innovation. Liquid is headquartered in Silicon Valley, where innovation is a way of life.

Neumeier divides his time at Liquid among three activities—shaping client engagements, writing books and articles on business and design, and giving workshops on brand strategy and design thinking. Outside of work he enjoys cooking (badly), keeping up with movies (barely), reading (business), and traveling with his wife Eileen to destinations that promise romance and good food. You can reach him through the Liquid Agency website at www.liquidagency.com.